Ruth

D1135090

I WAS JACQUELINE KENNEDY'S
DRESSMAKER

ALSO CO-AUTHORED BY FRANCES SPATZ LEIGHTON

White House Chef (with François Rysavy)

I Married The Veep (with Jane Hadley Barkley)

I Prayed Myself Slim (with Deborah Pierce)

Bum Voyage (with David Lee Greer, aged 10)

I Married a Psychiatrist (with Louise Pfister)

My Thirty Years Backstairs at the White House
(with Lillian Rogers Parks)

I Was Jacqueline Kennedy's Dressmaker

by

MINI RHEA

with

FRANCES SPATZ LEIGHTON

Fashion Drawings by
Mini Rhea with Sylvia Baptista

FLEET PUBLISHING CORPORATION
230 PARK AVENUE, NEW YORK 17, N.Y.

CONTENTS

Part 1. THE JACKIE I KNEW

This book is dedicated
to
my daughters Sylvia and Jimi,
who were my inspiration
through all the years

PREFACE

*I first met Mini Rhea after the 1960 election. She was
brought to my home and introduced to me by someone
who thought her story might be interesting for* The American Weekly, *of which I am the Washington Editor.*

*As I listened to her talk and heard her wonderful anec-
dotes of the days when, as a young girl, Jacqueline Bouvier
came tripping in to have new dresses made and old ones
altered, I wondered how all this wealth of material could
be squeezed into one magazine article.*

*It just couldn't. Jacqueline had meant too much to Mini
Rhea, not as a girl who was destined to become the most
important woman in our country, but as a warm human
being with a sense of humor so delightful that Mini had
saved many clippings of Jackie's newspaper career.*

*I laughed with Mini Rhea as I read Jacqueline's account
of her interview with gift wrappers at a department store
during the Christmas rush, amusingly illustrated by her
own drawings. One showed three clerks struggling to wrap
a baby grand piano, with one of the girls stranded up in
the air as the top of the piano flips open. The story told of*

many things, such as how "working the Christmas rush" is "what makes your feet get bigger" and how customers exasperatingly change their minds, in mid-wrap, about which paper they want and how they insist on choosing the unwrappable present. For example, foam rubber pillows. The wrapper who had battled with those told Jackie, "Those foam pillows . . . I thought had me beat. They kept popping out and hitting the ceiling. The man said he hoped they didn't scare his mother when she opened the package."

The article, from beginning to end, showed Jacqueline's wonderful eye for detail and her feeling for people. It even chronicled a touching moment when a customer had asked the wrapper to pick out a nice paper and ribbons for a corsage she handed her. When the expensive wrapping job was completed and paid for, the customer had handed the gift back to the wrapper and said, "That's for you. Merry Christmas!"

I remember a day I spent with Mrs. Kennedy at her Georgetown home when she was the wife of a Senator whom many said would be the next President. I, too, had been impressed with her sense of humor and her warmth. I remember she seemed much more interested in charitable work, such as helping retarded children, than she was in the social whirl.

We went that day to visit infants being cared for in foster homes under the auspices of the Washington Home for Foundlings. Jacqueline held these babies in her arms tenderly, as only someone with a deep love of children could do, and they reacted with happy gurgles. Everyone we came into contact with that day, from office workers in her husband's office to the cab driver who drove us to the foster home, seemed to respond to the quietly dressed Senator's wife. There was nothing high hat about her—

we perched on drug store stools at lunch time and had hamburgers.

Her house, too, was quietly and tastefully done, without ostentation, and a picture the photographer snapped that day became the one which Jacqueline used first at the White House when answering requests for autographed pictures of herself. It was made by Jacques Lowe, with whom Mrs. Kennedy spoke in French.

The story that I did with Mini Rhea entitled "The Start of the 'Jackie Look'" can be found in The American Weekly *of March 15, 1961.*

Mini Rhea turned out to be a modest and unassuming woman whose talent as a dressmaker had shown up surprisingly at the age of ten when she shocked her mother by cutting out a dress for herself without using a pattern. She had sewn nothing but doll clothes before that, but she quickly followed up her amazing feat by embarking on the job of re-designing her whole wardrobe and was soon doing the same for her older sisters.

When an infection following a vaccination threatened the loss of her arm, Mini had but one thought as the fever reached a dangerous stage—would she still be able to sew for her dolls with only one arm?

It was wonderfully fitting and touching that the little girl, who cared so much for designing and making doll clothes, should grow up to sew for a future First Lady.

—Frances Spatz Leighton
Washington, D.C.

I WAS JACQUELINE KENNEDY'S DRESSMAKER

PROLOGUE

**MINI RHEA
CUSTOM DRESSMAKER**

I WAS HOME AT LAST! How proud I was to direct the placement of my bronze plaque—"Mini Rhea, Custom Dressmaker"—beside the doorway of 1820 35th Street, N.W., a
typical flat-front Georgetown house. Some day, perhaps,
someone will put up another sign there: "Through this
door passed Jacqueline Kennedy."

But what a strange chain of circumstances led her to this
door.

I was working as a dressmaker in a sewing machine store
located four or five blocks from the White House, just to
learn the ropes in order to open my own shop later. But
I almost muffed my big chance, which came in the form

of a rotund maid who spoke with a Slavic accent. She kept seeking me out and asking me to come with her to the "Madame" because "The Madame will be so grateful. The old regular dressmaker, she die." I kept telling her that I was too busy to go. If "Madame" meant the same thing in the North as it did in the South, where I grew up, I just felt I would be better off without her business.

But finally I did promise to come see her "Madame." Thank the dear Lord I did, because "Madame" turned out to be one of the finest and most respectable leaders of Washington society. And she and her friends gave me enough work to get me started in my own shop. A long line of people eventually led me to Jacqueline Bouvier.

First I met Mrs. Neill Phillips. She recommended me to five friends—Mrs. Walter Lippmann, Mrs. Ella Burling, Mrs. Curtis Munson, Mrs. Blair Childs and, finally, Mrs. Arthur Krock. Mrs. Krock, wife of the noted newspaperman, in turn recommended me to a special friend of hers, Mrs. Hugh Auchincloss. And Mrs. Hugh Auchincloss eventually recommended me to her daughters, Caroline Lee and Jacqueline.

My Georgetown shop was the beginning of a wonderful new life. Rarely have I met a woman so sensitive and kind as Mrs. Auchincloss. She shopped in Georgetown but lived in nearby McLean, Virginia. She liked my work and her stamp of approval sent many of her Georgetown friends to my shop. My little place became a sub-station for the entire Auchincloss group. Though I worked hard, the relaxed atmosphere surrounding these charming women made it all seem like play or a pleasant hobby.

I found myself party to all their affairs of the day. I was included in their "happy talk." I knew who did what and when, who approved and who didn't, and I became as interested in the doings of their children as I was in the activities of my own.

I kept hearing about Jackie from her mother for several years before I set eyes on her. Jackie was here; Jackie was there. She was at the Sorbonne; she was at George Washington University. She was vacationing in New York, in Florida, in Europe. I decided she must keep her bags packed at all times.

Mrs. Auchincloss was so happy, in 1951, when she told me that her daughter Jacqueline had just won *Vogue's* coveted *Prix de Paris,* and I was just as pleased as she was, although I had not yet met "Jackie," as all her friends called her.

I was astounded that this George Washington senior had been able to capture the imagination of the hard-bitten editors, not only with the subject matter she covered, but also with her literary style. She wrote about three famous persons she wished she had known, and I was impressed with her maturity. I was familiar with only one of the three she wrote about—Oscar Wilde. The other two, Charles Baudelaire and Sergei Pavlovich Diaghilev, were completely unknown to me until that moment when I learned from Mrs. Auchincloss that Baudelaire was an 18th century French poet and Diaghilev was a famous Russian ballet impresario.

Mrs. Auchincloss told me about the technical papers on fashion which Jackie had also submitted to win the prize, and ended by saying that the winner was entitled to spend half a year in France, working on the Paris edition of *Vogue,* and half a year as a Junior Editor on *Vogue* in New York.

I was amazed to learn a little later that, because she had already spent a year studying at the Sorbonne, Jackie had decided not to take the year's job with *Vogue.* Had she accepted, it would have put her directly into the fashion field, just as it had twenty-three other young women then on the staff of *Vogue* or the other Condé Nast publications, who had been previous winners of the *Prix de Paris*.

I was even more amazed when Mrs. Auchincloss, after showing me a picture of Jacqueline, told me that she wanted to bring Jackie in to meet me, so that I could work with her on some of her fashion ideas. Me, working with a prize-winner in fashion? It made me a bit nervous even to think of it.

Mrs. Auchincloss put me at ease. "My daughter would just love you," she said. "She likes to design her own clothes and I know she would love to work with someone like you who could help her with them."

—MINI RHEA

CHAPTER 1

A NEW CUSTOMER TAKES THE PRIZE

I WAITED NERVOUSLY for the prize-winning fashion expert to come in. She had made her own appointment by telephone and as soon as I heard her voice my mind flashed the signal "finishing school." Many of my customers had gone to finishing school, but this voice had something beside the perfect tones, soft modulation and self-confidence of private school training. The added ingredient was gentleness—even on the phone she sounded warm and kind. And she sounded in a hurry, something my finishing school products never admitted to.

It was a Saturday and I tried to get my daughters from underfoot, but fourteen-year-old Sylvia and especially twelve-year-old Jimi could almost smell excitement and gravitated to it like moths around a flame.

"Who is coming?" they demanded.

"Just a girl who won a prize on a fashion magazine. You wouldn't be interested," I told them.

"Then why are you all excited?" they asked.

"I'm not excited," I said. "I'm just nervous because I'm not used to people from the fashion world."

"What about that woman who owns a whole dress shop and still she brings *you* her dresses to make?"

"That's different," I explained. "She just *sells clothes*."

"Oh Mother," said Sylvia, "you used to be so impressed about that. I don't know what to make of you."

"But this girl actually *designs* dresses. Now you two just go outside or upstairs or downstairs, wherever you want to be, or you'll be trapped. Now scoot."

The girls had orders to stay out of the living room when I was fitting a customer there because it also served as my fitting room. If one was trapped in the kitchen, fixing a sandwich or getting a coke, when a customer arrived, she was supposed to stay there until the customer left. It was the rule.

The girls went outside and, glancing out the window, I could see they were standing around to get a glimpse of the girl who could make their mother nervous.

Jackie came dashing in, laden with dresses, fashion magazines and a sketch pad. She was as gracious as her mother, as she explained that the ready-made dresses needed some alterations in the waistline and the bustline. After showing the dresses to me, she brought out her own sketches—if they could be called sketches. "Squiggles" would be more appropriate.

"Mother recommended you highly, Mrs. Rhea, and said you'd be able to understand what I want," Jackie said with a warm little smile, looking a bit shy and uncertain.

"Well, I'll do the best I can," I said. "I have a feeling I can learn a lot more from you than you can from me. *You* won the prize."

"Yes, but *you* do the actual doing," she said.

I invited her to sit down and we talked a while about what she had done to win *Vogue's Prix de Paris*. I was very

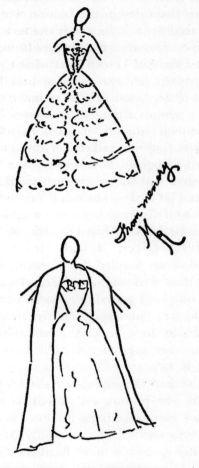

Here is the way Jackies
squiggled dress designs
looked. This one is drawn
from memory.

curious because it was my secret dream someday to be a full-fledged dress designer.

Jackie told me a little about the articles on fashion she had submitted, along with the profiles of the three persons she wished she had known. But what especially fascinated me was that she had also submitted the layout for a whole issue of *Vogue*. Good grief, I thought, she's a dynamo—about five persons wrapped up in one.

I was much amused to learn that her mother, Mrs. Auchincloss, had first talked her into entering the contest and then had helped talk her out of accepting the prize.

"Of course I made up my own mind," she said, "but I have spent a lot of time abroad. It's time I settled down and thought about doing something constructive. And I do get lonely for the family when I'm away so long."

"But it's a career," I said. "It's a chance to have a wonderful career handed to you on a silver platter."

How I longed to take her place, accept the prize for her. Oh, how quickly I would have accepted, had I been young as she and without responsibilities. Six months in Paris, six months in New York! She had won over some 1,500 contestants, her mother had told me, and here she was throwing it away.

"Oh, I've had the experience of it," Jackie said. "That was t-rrific (she pronounced it as if it had no "e") but I don't know about making a career of fashion. It's more of a hobby with me."

Her voice was even more unusual now that I heard it without the distortion of the phone. It had a liquid sound, like water cascading. And it had a sound of suppressed laughter, as if at any moment she might break out into ripples of hilarity.

What an unusual girl she was and what an unusual voice. I tried to keep her talking so that I could enjoy listening to her longer. I wondered if she had ever thought of radio or

TV as a career, but I didn't ask. Anyone who would turn down a fashion career was automatically beyond my comprehension. But I determined to find out what made her tick.

As Jackie went behind the screen to change into one of the dresses she had brought for remodelling, I thought of how surprised she would be if she knew how much I already knew about her and the other members of her family, especially her younger sister Lee—little things I had learned from her mother and other customers who were her friends.

For example, I had heard of the time that Lee, who was three-and-a-half years younger, had captured the spotlight at Jackie's coming-out party. I should say *one* of her coming-out parties, because I knew she had been introduced to society at Newport, Rhode Island; Tuxedo, New York; New York City, and finally at McLean, Virginia.

It had happened at the Newport party in the famous Clambake Club. Jackie had worn a demure, proper, puff-sleeved and bouffant white gown, just as every young deb should wear, when suddenly fourteen-year-old Lee made a grand entrance, like a movie star, in a strapless, shimmering gown she had smuggled in somehow, and stole the show and the stag line too. Poor Jackie was fit to be tied, but Mrs. Auchincloss enjoyed the humor of the situation and laughingly took it in stride.

Just as there was a *Compleat Angler,* to my mind Mrs. Auchincloss was, of all my customers, the *Compleat Mother.* Without in the least smothering them, she took an intense interest in her children and gloried in each of their triumphs, small or large. It was her sense of humor about them which helped her with the problems of adjusting the home life of three separate sets of children. First there were Jackie and Lee, the children of her first husband, Jack Bouvier, a Wall Street broker, for whom Jackie

... her white tulle coming out dress. But this
earlier gown had been artless and almost
unadorned. It was the perfect dress to set off
the beauty of Jacqueline at seventeen, budding
into womanhood

was named. Then there were Janet and James Auchincloss, the two children of her second marriage. Finally, there were Tom, Nina and Hugh, Jr.—the one affectionately known as Yusha—the children of Hugh Auchincloss by his two previous marriages.

Somehow Mrs. Auchincloss maintained a happy, easy-going household, and when she was in for a fitting she was forever reaching for my phone to check on how the children were making out at home or arranging to pick up this one here or that one there. She was completely wrapped up in the young ones and relished their every adventure.

Jackie seems to have been the most colorful child of the family, surviving many a calamity—falling off a horse, getting lost at the age of two. On that occasion, the story goes, she had simply gone up to a policeman and reported that her *nurse* was lost.

From what I understood, Jackie had always been an amazing student. Her mother hadn't even realized that she knew how to read until one day, when Jackie was about six, she suddenly surprised Mrs. Auchincloss by talking about a story she had read all by herself. At school she got almost straight A's without much effort. As a matter of fact, her exertions seemed to center on tomboy pranks in the schools she attended and, consequently, she was always in hot water.

She was a ringleader at the proper Miss Porter's school in Farmington, Connecticut, in such activities as swiping extra food and staging snack parties after "lights out." But both she and the school had survived. However, the head-mistress had once told Mrs. Auchincloss that the thing which had saved prankster Jacqueline was the fact that she had one of the most inquiring minds the school had ever known.

Jackie had also survived Lee's effort to upstage her at

her own coming out party and had, in fact, in 1948 been named Debutante of the Year by Cholly Knickerbocker, the New York society writer. He had commented that Jacqueline Bouvier was the first debutante to deserve the crown since it had been worn by Brenda Frazier a few years earlier.

Someone had given me that clipping in 1948 when it appeared in Cholly Knickerbocker's column, and as I looked at Jackie emerging from behind the gray-patterned screen which blended with the mural on my wall, I had to agree with Igor Cassini, the man behind the "Cholly" pen name, that Jacqueline looked regal enough to be "Queen of the Debutantes." "Dresden porcelain," he had called her, and she was exactly that.

Looking back, it amuses me that it is Igor Cassini's brother, Oleg Cassini, who was chosen to be Jacqueline's official designer and clothes co-ordinator as soon as she became America's First Lady. It is so typical of the Auchincloss family to become attached to various persons and their relatives and to maintain their loyalty to them for many years. I was glad to be a part of their way of life, with its wide horizons, many friends—and loyalty.

In her old pictures I noticed that debutante Jackie had worn her hair like Brenda Frazier's, parted on the side and pulled flat across the top of the head. She had also tucked it behind one ear part of the time, in the approved Frazier glamor look. But as she came toward me I noticed she had graduated to a more casual flyaway feather cut. Though she was tall—five foot, seven—on her it looked properly proportioned and individualistic.

She had a figure like a model, long and lean. I knew that once she had been chubby, but no one could accuse her of that now. Her neck was swan-like—a portrait painter's delight—perfect, and she held her head high. Her arms and back were lovely. She had the long legs that are the American ideal. I thought what a lucky girl she was.

"How would you like this fixed?" I asked and found that Jackie wanted her waist nipped in more and the bustline more emphasized.

"Don't worry," I said. "I have a magic dart which does wonders and I know you'll like it."

"T-rrific," she said.

Next I got ready to translate her sketch into a gown. She explained exactly what each squiggle meant—a seam here, a swoosh of the skirt to the back, and a tricky banding there at the top of the bodice—and soon I found myself caught up in her enthusiasm and telling her, quite excitedly for me, how the dress could be made.

I was surprised at how sketchy her sketch was, but I asked her to remove her dress and slip so that I could make my muslin pattern. Then it was Jackie's turn to be surprised. "How in the world do you do that?" she asked.

I had to admit that I had developed my own technique for giving a dress a perfect fit. This was to make, first, a muslin skin-tight covering on the person I was fitting. This established the figure in all its proportions and disproportions. Then I always cut out in muslin the pattern of each individual dress.

"This is how I know what I'm doing when I cut into the good material," I said, "and I see that you really know good material." She had brought some beautiful heavy white embroidered satin.

"It came from France," she said, smiling at my appreciation.

I tried to determine the color of Jackie's eyes. They defied definition. They looked light brown, yet they had other colors in them too, and seemed almost hazel. Later I was to see them described as anything from light brown to gray-green.

"Where did you get your training in dressmaking, Mrs. Rhea?" Jackie asked.

"I didn't. I've never had a course but I'm not proud of it. Actually, the only training I've had is a course in hat making which I took a few years ago. I had a notion I might like to go into the hat business."

"Well, if you had, I wouldn't be here," she said emphatically. "I can't get excited about hats. They complicate a costume and take away from the look of unity."

"You hate hats?"

"No, that's a strong word. Let's say they're fine for church."

Taffy, my taffy-colored cocker, ambled over and bumped into Jackie, almost forcing her off balance.

"I'm so sorry," I said. "Taffy, go sit down."

Jackie, unlike so many other customers, was instantly on the side of the dog. "Oh, what a cute dog," she said, "but what's wrong with her?"

"Not a thing except she's going blind. Some people think we should have her put away or given to some scientific institution or something."

Jackie was horrified. "Oh, I hope you never will," she protested. "Taffy's a wonderful dog." She knelt to get a better look. "She's t-rrific."

As Taffy responded to her gentle words and petting, Jackie told me how, when she was a little girl, she and Lee had written a letter to a newspaper about being kind to dogs. "We were living in New York then," she added. "Of course, Daddy helped us write it."

The way she spoke her father's name showed her great warmth toward him. I knew that Jackie felt very close to her father and visited him whenever she could. He was her real hero, who shared her innermost thoughts and understood her restless spirit. But Lee was more like her mother, I had been told, very quiet and feminine and, incidentally, always more interested in clothes than Jackie was.

I also had the impression that Jackie was really surprised that she had won the *Prix de Paris,* but that it had given her new confidence in her own taste in clothes, as if she had finally earned the right to make her own judgments.

I was to see that confidence grow.

I continued to pin the muslin in place so that it formed almost a second skin. (To make a skin-tight muslin form for yourself, see the directions I have given on page 321 in Part II.) While working, I commented on how lucky Jacqueline was to have a figure like a model right out of a Parisian salon of *haute couture.*

But I was amazed to learn that Jackie didn't think she was perfect or ideal, and in fact was quite critical of herself. She wished her feet were smaller, her waist slimmer, her bust were larger, her legs were straighter and her face more oval.

I felt like spanking her. Here she stood—the most beautiful girl who had walked through my door—and she was beset by small dissatisfactions, just like anyone else. "If I had your face and form I think I'd head for Hollywood," I said.

"Or home," she said, laughing. "I'm late."

At least, I thought, this girl will never be conceited.

I unpinned her and, when she returned all dressed again, I noted her poise and perfect carriage. This is the secret of elegance, I thought. No one looking at her would suspect for a moment that she was less than supremely confident or completely satisfied with herself. There was a lesson here for my girls when they would be older, I mused. I would tell them, "First you must know your own good points and bad. Then it is up to you to make the most of the good ones and rise above the bad ones. Don't let others see your disappointments. The important thing is to present a picture of confidence and serenity to the world."

I asked Jackie to sign my guest book. She wrote in a strong, artistic hand: "November 3, 1951. Jacqueline Bouvier, Merrywood, McLean, Virginia, WO–4020."

Guests

Date	Name	Residence
Nov. 1	Ho W F Chappell III	4632 Conn St.,	
Nov 3rd	Jacqueline Bouvier	Merrywood–McLean Va – WO-4020
Nov. 9	Elizabeth Cosgrove 1200-16 N.W.	District of Columbia Republic 3
Nov. 10	Helen Robin 1255 Connecticut NE 3
Nov. 10	May Pettit 5210 Fulton Rd	Bethesda, Md.
Nov. 12	Barbara Linafter 2501 Que St, Apt 5,	Du 901
Nov. 13	Sly Mead 2615 42nd N.W.	1152
Nov. 13	Mrs R Chusmith 1 Wordham Rd Md Wis 5861
Nov. 13	Margaret Fowler 314 27th Street Ca 5590

I knew that number by heart. When I had things ready for Mrs. Auchincloss I would use it to telephone her. Merrywood was the huge, many-acred estate of Hugh D. Auchincloss, with many rooms, many servants, a tennis court and a swimming pool. I had other customers with equally lavish estates and it was the bane of my existence that when I called such homes the servants seemed bent on keeping me from talking to the mistress of the house. But the Auchincloss household was different. The butler would recognize my voice and in a most friendly way would put me through to Mrs. Auchincloss immediately.

Sometimes I could hear the dogs barking on the other end of the line, and they seemed friendly too. My own dog, Taffy, sitting on my lap, would cock her little head and bark right back. We would laugh and conclude our phone conversation in refined pandemonium.

I'd had such an interesting time with Jackie, I hated to see her go. As I saw her gather up her things and leave as quickly as she had come, I thought, this girl is unusual. This girl, I hope will come often.

The big news of the day was the visit of Princess Elizabeth in Washington. She had dined with President and Mrs. Truman at Blair House. She was on her way to Canada. How could I guess—how in my wildest dreams could I foresee—that this girl sitting on *my* sofa, standing at *my* mirror, walking to *my* door and turning to bid *me* a smiling goodbye, would herself some day be entertaining royalty in the White House.

How?

Such ideas would have made the plot of a fairy tale!

THE START OF THE JACKIE LOOK

A FAMILIAR PATTERN soon evolved—Jackie would dash in and show me a design.

"I have a t-rrific idea for a gown. I think it should have this kind of a top," she would say as she pulled out a mere suggestion of a sketch. "The skirt should be like this," she would add, doodling with her pencil. "You understand, don't you, Mrs. Rhea?"

And, of course, I did. Between the two of us we would soon crystallize the idea of how the dress should be made.

While I draped the muslin she would often look down at me and say, "I don't know how in the world you know what you're doing, but I know you do."

I would laugh and say, "This is as clear to me as your sketches are to you."

Jacqueline shared my love for fabulous materials and colors. Quite frequently she brought me materials that had come from abroad and together we would work out a design.

Jackie could tell by the feel of a fabric whether it would

make up well. She never liked sleazy materials, or ones that looked cheaply made, with no body or finish to them. She would handle a fabric and say, "This feels good; it will make up well."

Jackie never wore chiffon or ultra-clinging material. She liked materials with more body. Even years later, at the Inaugural Ball of 1961, I noticed the chiffon in her gown and cape were over heavier material.

She wore a lot of black, in suits and daytime clothes, but not so much for evening. Pink—hot pink—was her favorite color, to match her lipstick. I noticed her beautiful, long eyelashes. Her complexion had a transparency; it was so perfect and her skin tones were warm, blending well with her chestnut brown hair. The pink she liked so well did the most for her coloring.

Jackie began coming to the shop with a lot of sewing. She paid me one of her nicest compliments when we were working against a deadline to finish a dress for a certain affair. She was starting to say that maybe it wouldn't be ready, then she stopped and smiled. "I don't know why I'm worrying. I should know by now that when you say you'll do something, you'll do it, or else!"

She was a joy to work with for she could look at something and make a quick decision—yes—no. A little higher—an inch more to the right.

Other customers would sometimes come back endlessly, complaining, "It still isn't right. I think I want it this way instead." But not Jackie. She would say, "It's t-rrific!" It was her special expression.

The way muslin could be used to decide exactly what cut looked best on a person fascinated Jackie. One day, muffled in muslin, with her head sticking out of a small opening, she experimented with necklines and shoulder-lines.

"I definitely look better with this sleeveless effect," she said, looking in the mirror.

"Yes," I commented, seeing what she meant. "It's a pity the style isn't that way for daytime."

Jackie excused herself and got a magazine from her stack of things on the couch. It was my first good look at a French fashion magazine.

"Look in here, Mrs. Rhea." She flipped open a few pages. "Look at the variety. You'll find almost any look you want. Why can't you wear a sleeveless dress for daytime?"

"I don't know why," I said. "It just isn't being done."

As I leafed through the magazine, amazed at the galaxy of clothes the French were wearing and the extreme look of French dresses, Jackie stood working with the muslin at the neck and shoulder, determining how deep a scoop looked good on her and how deep an armhole should be cut.

"Yes," she said, "I like the slim sleeveless look. I think the shoulder should come about here." She pointed to the tip of the shoulder bone. "And I think it should barely cover the neck bone here," as she ran her finger along the ridge of the bone.

Some time later, as if to test out her theory, she ordered such a dress for daytime and I remember I suggested a little jacket to cover her arms.

"No, that would be losing the whole point," she said. "I'll just have the dress."

Even in November 1951, when Jackie first came to my shop, I noticed that her tastes were different from the average. She seemed to ignore the fads of the moment. Slave bracelets on ankles were a big thing—she wore none. Hair looked harshly pulled back, with nary a curl on the forehead. Jackie would try to soften her forehead line. Choker beads, tight around the throat, of two, three and

even four strands, were almost a uniform—even with sports clothes. Jackie never wore them, preferring the more dignified look of a longer single or double strand of pearls softening the neckline of the dress.

Platform shoes and open-toed ones were *big*—but not with Jackie.

The general style for dresses at the time was: a big skirt, becoming wider at the hem, a few inches above the ankle; sweetheart or scalloped necklines; big loose cape sleeves. Puff sleeves were common too, but sleeveless dresses were unheard of. There was a general Southern belle look about most dresses, particularly as they were gathered into a tight waist. The materials were soft and had little body.

This was certainly not the Jackie look. Jackie, even then, insisted on cleaner, neater, more compact lines and material with firmer body, so that the garments would hold their shape.

Jackie started shortening her dresses before any of my other customers. "An inch off can make all the difference," she said.

I was to learn that, though Jacqueline Bouvier's ideas seemed a little strange at the time she voiced them, I would hear more about them later from New York designers and smart specialty shops and, eventually, from the general public.

Somehow, in following her own thinking, she seemed always to be a little ahead of fashion's decrees. Some people are fashion followers. Jackie was never intimidated into wearing what others were wearing. Some sixth sense told her where fashion's trend was leading.

Maybe, in studying the French fashion magazines, she was guided by instinct to know which of the styles would survive. I don't know. But I *do* know that I soon realized that, if I saw some new idea on Jackie, I would eventually find it becoming the accepted mode. She was the first of my customers to nip her skirts in below the hipline, while everyone else was wearing them wide or gored. It was several years before others were demanding the "tapered look."

And because of Jackie, I began buying French fashion magazines myself. I studied the pictures, which was almost as fruitful as if I had been able to read their French captions. *L'Officiel* was one of her favorites, and *L'Art et la Mode*. I also got one named *Femina luxe*. And of course, there was the French edition of *Vogue*.

It was an expensive habit to become addicted to, because French fashion magazines in America cost something like $10 an issue. It was a blessing that they did not come out monthly, but only for each season.

Jackie would try to talk me into studying French so that I could understand the French approach better. "You could make it a family affair and just talk French at the table." She told me how she had gotten practice in conversation at home where, at certain meals, if you forgot and spoke a word of English you had to forfeit a coin.

I determined I would study French one day—and I'm *still* determined.

I noticed that Jackie backed away from certain colors—green, gold, yellow and brown. She liked white, beige and black, pale yellow and, of course, pink—the brighter, the better.

I nearly always wore red dresses on bad weather days to lift my own morale and that of my customers. Jackie said once, "I love to see you in red. It does something for my spirits on this foul day."

She told me how it had depressed her as a child to have to wear a school uniform with its sameness of color and I told her how I had had an opposite experience while in school.

As a senior in high school, it was forcefully demonstrated

to me what the proper dress could do for one. I was com-
peting in a regional piano contest—the previous year I had
only won third place, and this year my teacher was determined that I would win first place. A few days before the
event, when I had rehearsed my piece, "La Fille aux
Cheveau de Lin" (The Maid with the Flaxen Hair) for
what seemed the millionth time, she asked me what I was
going to wear. The dress I described must have sounded
very uninteresting, for she said, "Oh, no, you are going to
wear a dress that I will lend you." It turned out to be a
bright red chiffon, with a lovely full skirt, and the minute
I put it on I felt as confident as she that I would win, and
I did!

"That's t-rrific," she said. "I guess red does the same
thing for you that pink does for me. I always feel so good
in it. Like anything's possible."

"It's really your color," I agreed.

The major problems Jacqueline had in dressing were
her wide, wide-set eyes and the rather square cut of her
face. Because of these features she had to avoid square
necklines, square shoulders and squarish hairdos which
would make her eyes look still further apart and her face
more squarish. She needed and used a slanting or irregular
line in her hairdo or dress. Sometimes she achieved the
off-center effect merely with a brooch on the shoulder.

I would notice, when her hair was pulled completely off
her forehead, that it was not a good style for her. She
definitely looked best when at least a few locks of hair
swept over the forehead with an irregular effect.

Once, to achieve the off-center effect, Jackie designed an
evening gown with an ornamental design sweeping from
the strapless top down one side to the floor. But she did
not like to get the effect with side drapes or bunching of
the material because that would ruin the simple lines she

preferred. She did not wear fluffy things—she didn't wear "buttons and bows."

But like a true individualist, once she had made her rules, she would break them at least once to see the result. She didn't like ruffles, but once she wore a ruffle all the way down the side of the dress. As this was the only ornamentation, the effect was not bad. Then she had one dress with a button on each shoulder. It made her wide-set eyes look too far apart, so it was not a good idea.

However, the wonderful thing about Jackie's eyes was that with the right hairdo they were her most exciting and beautiful feature and set her completely apart from anyone else. If any one feature made her memorable, it was her lovely brownish hazel eyes.

I'll never forget the experience I had with one of Jackie's dresses. It caused me to look upon her more as a friend than as a customer.

It was in early December, 1951, when she rushed in with a sketch, yards of bright pink peau de soie and yards and yards of silver braid. The braid was on two big spindles, and I could feel my eyesight going as I looked at it. Her design, as we finally worked it out, called for a strapless dress, very fitted, with a very full skirt and a difficult design of braid sewn in absolutely straight lines all over it. Jackie needed the dress for a special occasion and I promised to have it finished in time for her to pick it up the morning of the event.

Suddenly both of my daughters became desperately ill with a virus infection. I remember I was sitting sewing on the braid in the living room, the night before the dress was due, with the dress draped over the ironing board. The silver line stretched on endlessly. Before my weary eyes the pattern looked like a maze from which I would never find my way out. The glitter of the silver played tricks with my eyes. First it sparkled like a thousand constellations in the sky; then it writhed like a snake that I had to keep fighting off; then again, it danced like a flickering fire. Why, oh why, I asked myself, did I ever get into this dressmaking business? Surely there must be some other way to support my daughters. I was starting to feel the "or else" Jackie had referred to had finally arrived.

Every once in awhile I went in to look at the girls, because I was worried about their illness. At about eleven o'clock they both seemed much worse and I called the doctor for them. I was grateful that he came on that cold, sleety night.

When he was ready to leave, he glanced at the billows of pink and silver on my ironing board in the living room. "Are you still working?" he asked. Then, looking at me searchingly, "How do you feel?"

"All right," I answered, "except that I'm worried about the girls and I have to finish this dress before tomorrow morning."

He left, shaking his head doubtfully.

I finished the dress, but I woke up at five o'clock in the morning—only a few hours after I had gone to bed—and called the doctor for myself. Again he came through the cold at an unearthly hour and found the girls improving, but ordered me to stay in bed.

Jacqueline arrived jauntily some hours later to pick up the dress. She put it on and came to my bedroom to show me how it looked. I tried to keep her out, for fear she might catch my virus, but she insisted that didn't worry her. In fact, she sat down on the edge of my bed to chat and keep me company.

Never before had such a thing happened to me—a customer sitting on my bed, taking such a personal interest and with such concern for my welfare. I felt a little choked up —and it wasn't all due to my cold. Soon I was forgetting all about my misery and laughing uproariously at her tales of adventures in Europe. How she had hung from the heels and had kissed the Blarney Stone. How on her first trip to Europe with a bunch of college girls she had spent half her nights in the bathroom washing clothes. "We never got out of the bathroom any night," she said. "When I think of our wasted bathroom nights . . ." she added, and we both laughed as she left the sentence suspended.

She told me how she had tried to make up for those wasted nights when she took her sister, Lee, along on her third trip to Europe. I was no longer in my sick bed, but strolling down the streets of Paris, surrounded by flower stalls, so vividly did she describe the scenes. The flowers of Europe had made a great impression on her and on me also as she talked about them. Real? I could almost smell them. And in my mind's eye I sat at a sidewalk cafe, sipping an *aperitif,* and lamenting with her that Washington, D.C., had none of these charming outdoor cafes. We agreed it was practically a crime.

She had gone to Europe the first time, for six weeks, the summer after her freshman year at college. She went with three friends. Two of them were stepdaughters of Ed Foley, Undersecretary of the Treasury. At a garden party given by Queen Elizabeth, the girls had cornered Winston Churchill and chatted with him. And then had come the biggest thrill—a nod from the Queen.

The second time Jackie went abroad was during her junior year, which she spent studying at the Sorbonne. And what studying! With winter gloves on. She lived with a refined French family who were in straightened circumstances, and therefore could not afford much heat. Jackie said that she often had to do her studying bundled up like an Egyptian mummy. But she learned to speak French fluently.

When she talked about animals—real or imagined—she was aglow. There was a brown bear that she "thought" lived with her when she was a little girl and there was a very real horse named "Danseuse" which she *wanted* to have come live with her when she went to Miss Porter's, or "Farmington" as she called it, after the school's location.

Had she taken the horse, I wanted to know.

I should have known the answer was "yes." She had simply talked her grandfather Bouvier into supporting the horse for her at school. "I paid Grampy with poems," she said. "Or shall I call a bribe a bribe?"

"I wish I could bribe you to be my doctor," I said. "I feel a hundred per cent better just listening to you." She had a way of talking that compelled you to listen—both to what she said and to the rippling waterfall voice that said it.

I thanked her for lifting my mind from myself and my miseries.

"I should be thanking you for working on my dress when you must have felt miserable," she said. "You shouldn't have done it. But I'll think about you when I wear it tonight and I know it will make my Christmas holidays."

After she left I worried a while in case she would catch my cold and then, that night, I got word that my mother had died in Gulfport, Mississippi, my birthplace, where she had returned to spend the latter years of her life. It was December 6, 1951.

The First Lady will learn here for the first time that that date, December 6, 1951, is engraved on my memory forever, with its jumble of sickness, doctor, news of my dear mother's death, pink dress stretched out on the ironing board, silver braid curling around and around—and mixed with it all, her kindness.

The pink of this special dress, I soon began to realize,

was her special trademark. There was bound to be a pink—generally a bright pink—dress in every batch of clothes she bought on a shopping trip and brought to me for remodeling.

Right after the 1951 Christmas holidays, I noticed a lovely ring on Jackie's engagement finger, and asked her about it. She told me that she had just become engaged to John Husted of New York, but that the announcement was still to be made.

He had been educated in England, and at St. Paul's School in Concord, New Hampshire, and at Yale. He had been a Marine in the service—in Europe, and in India. He was the son of a New York banker. He had everything a parent could desire for a daughter—including good looks.

I heard of this engagement from another source too, a customer who was Mr. Husted's aunt—Mrs. Ellery Husted. Mrs. Husted was very pleased at the idea of Jackie becoming a part of her family.

For the next few months Jackie was very busy commuting back and forth to New York. She travelled so much she often paid me in travellers checks. But she didn't seem excited enough. I had the feeling Jackie had decided it was time for her to be serious and was trying to let her head rule her heart.

And two or three months later I discovered, one day, that the ring was not on her finger. I hesitated to ask, but she volunteered that she had just decided to call it off. That was in the early spring.

I wasn't surprised. Jackie hadn't looked too happy about her long distance courtship. "Too much long distance," she said. Mr. Husted would come to Washington one week end and Jackie would go to New York on alternate week ends. The plan had been, when the engagement was announced on January 21, 1952, for them to be married in June.

But by the time the engagement was broken, Jackie seemed more relieved than unhappy about it. Anyway, she didn't have time for tears, because she had gotten herself a brand new, glamorous job—that of an inquiring photographer.

---❦{ CHAPTER 3 }❦---

THROUGH THESE DOORS PASS . . .

WE USED TO HAVE a little saying in our workshop—"Another satisfied customer going to the White House in a Necchi gown."

This was said laughingly because Necchi was not the name of a famous dress designer, but of a new kind of zigzag sewing machine, of which we had one of the first in town. This was our way of bragging humorously about how many of our customers went to the White House.

Actually, we had two Necchis. I sat at one and my helper, Margy, sat at the other, and between the two machines sat the telephone on a stand. Sometimes we sewed with one hand and held the phone with the other.

I tried to have Margy do most of the answering because I was too busy with fittings and sewing, but even when I was with other customers the caller would usually insist upon a few words with me for reassurance about what to wear and how she looked in this or that dress, and would I really have a certain dress done on time, and so forth.

45

I would get disgusted about taking time for this type of customer baby-sitting.

A typical caller would start in briskly, sometimes breathlessly, "I'm going to the White House for a luncheon next week and I want to look right. What do you think I should wear? Do you think the silk suit you're doing is the proper thing?"

I'd say, "Yes. That would be fine for the White House luncheon because Mrs. Truman wears suits like that all the time."

The customer would think for a moment and then start arguing the merits of a print dress that hung in her closet—"Or should you make me a new dress?" She would keep me on the phone half an hour debating the pros and cons.

One person who never asked what she should wear was Jackie. She always knew what she was going to wear. And, anyway, she wasn't going to the White House—not in those days. We used to joke as we sat at our tandem sewing machines, that we wished Jackie *would* be invited to the White House—"Then we'd get some new customers, the way *she'd* look in her Necchi gown."

"Well," I commented to Margy, "the outlook for that isn't too bright. Mrs. Auchincloss is a Republican and the chances are all the family are Republicans, and the only way Jackie might be invited would be if Ike runs on the Republican ticket."

Even down-under, in our basement workroom, we were quite aware of, and interested in, Washington politics.

Really, though, our workshop was a very lovely recreation room, which was originally the downstairs dining room, with French doors that opened onto a typical Georgetown back yard, which had also been converted—into a charming patio. A fireplace at one end of the room added an Early American touch and we would keep it burning cheerfully at the slightest drop of the thermometer.

I had a dress form on my right as I sewed on my zig-zag machine and I would flip a garment over it quickly to see if it was draping properly. On my left sat Margy at the standard Necchi. Behind us were two other machines. One was a power machine—a high speed Singer that I trusted only myself to use. The other Singer was a blind stitch machine which I used for finishing.

We were very proud of our wonderful equipment.

I also had a portable Singer, which I carried for an emergency call to some socialite's home or to the home of some Congressman's wife, sometimes on the day of that much anticipated—and occasionally much dreaded—White House invitation.

I used to rejoice that *I* wasn't invited to the White House. It would have been too nerve-racking for me. You'd have to have nerves of steel, or poise like Jackie's, to cope with it, I'd reflect. I would wonder if the First Lady, Mrs. Truman, was as nervous about greeting her visitors as they were about meeting her.

I never saw Jackie excited in the slightest, except once, and even then I was amazed, under the circumstances, at how little agitated she was. She came hurrying in and asked quickly, "Mrs. Rhea, where can I get a pitcher of water?" I pointed to the kitchen. She was in and out in a minute, carrying the water and heading out the front door.

Curious to know who needed water, I ran to the door in time to see her calmly pouring the water into her car—through the window. Smoke billowed out.

"I set my car on fire with a cigarette," she said, smiling, as she passed me on her way to the kitchen again. "I think one more pitcher and I won't have to call the fire department."

Talk about calm in the face of conflagration!

Some of my customers became more excited just talking about a dress. And *their* cigarettes endangered *my* furniture every day—especially my pride and joy, the blond Wurlitzer piano which stood against the wall directly behind the customers as they gazed at themselves in the mirror.

For some reason the women seemed to smoke even more than usual during their fittings. And they were always backing away and leaning against the Wurlitzer as they studied themselves. It was bad enough that they were smoking while I was fitting them and there was danger of their putting a nice round hole through an unfinished dress, but I feared for my piano because they insisted on putting down their cigarette on the edge "for just a minute."

My approach to this problem was not too subtle. It was to put enough ash trays on that piano so that they could not possibly miss them. The piano top, covered with ceramic and glass ash trays, looked more like a bar top. I wish I had a picture of a customer with her friends and advisers pressing around—against the piano—all studying the reflection in the mirror and groping blindly behind them to reach the ash trays.

I think one of the first things that endeared Jacqueline Bouvier to me was that she very seldom smoked during a fitting. She, too, was afraid of burning a hole in a fine fabric.

There was another hazard in my fitting room—three windows across the front. I had provided a screen for customers to stand behind while dressing and undressing, but it proved to be more ornamental than useful because few of them used it and I was forever having to adjust the blinds to protect them from view. Though I managed to protect them from the public gaze, it did nothing for my eyesight, because sometimes I would find myself groping around in semi-darkness in the middle of the day.

To the left of the piano was a great big couch which faced the fireplace at the back end of the living room. As I had my fittings I would lay the dresses along that couch. With certain customers I would have to take the dresses out of sight because they would be nosy and inquisitive about them and inspect them carefully, asking whose they were and where they were to be worn. And if there were any price tags on dresses that had been bought in stores and were at my place for alteration, they would take a quick look at them also.

But Jackie would never go over to them, considering them none of her business. She might glance at them from a distance and make a comment, such as, "What a lovely shade of pink" or "I like that blue material. I've been hunting for something like that."

The Cadillacs would line up in front of my house and the chauffeurs would stand talking to one another. I tried to work by appointment only, but sometimes these women felt that schedules were made to be broken and some of them preferred to come at the same time so they could combine fittings with a friendly visit.

I remember Mrs. Styles Bridges' chauffeur because he was more attentive to his mistress than any other driver. I remember how he would run to meet her at the door to protect her with an umbrella if it even *looked* like rain.

Some of my customers insisted that I go to them and would send their chauffeurs for me. One of them was Mrs. Averell Harriman, whose husband held many positions throughout the Truman Administration, including that of Secretary of Commerce.

Mrs. Harriman sometimes sent a White House car to get me. The Harrimans had a private line connecting with the White House in their bedroom, and sometimes when

I was fitting Mrs. Harriman she would excuse herself to talk with Mrs. Truman. They would hold long, animated conversations about their various plans and I could see they were close friends.

Quite a few of my customers would invite me to various affairs. And one very important woman was kind enough always to invite me to fashion shows. One time it was for a luncheon fashion show at the Shoreham and her chauffeur came for me.

He seemed very embarrassed, I noticed, and when we got to the Shoreham he did not take me to the door but dropped me off on the street. "I'm terribly sorry," he said, "but Mrs. Blank Blank called me from downtown while I was washing the car and I didn't have time to change into my uniform. You're a fashion lady, so you can understand how I wouldn't want anyone seeing me like this in the Caddy. Would you mind walking just this little way?"

Talk about clothes-conscious *women!*

"How will Mrs. Blank Blank get here?" I asked.

"She said just to look after you and she'd hop a taxi."

One of my chauffeur-driven customers always brought along a little mesh bag with a square flat bottom and set it on my mantle while I was fitting her. I noticed, too, that she seemed to be addressing an occasional remark to it, in an undertone, and I wondered, What is it? Is it a bird?

Imagine my shock when I was informed by her maid that in the mesh bag, in a small box, were the ashes of the lady's husband, and that she took them with her everywhere she went! At home she had a place set for her departed spouse at every meal.

I hardly think it any wonder that, except for the one loyal maid, she had a hard time keeping servants. I must admit that I felt a little queer after that whenever she came for a fitting.

I also had a British customer, who had spent most of her lifetime in South Africa, who never went anywhere without her umbrella. No matter if the sun were shining, if it was hot, cool, or otherwise, she was always seen with her umbrella.

"Americans don't seem to care whether it's raining or shining," she said one day. "And they seem to ignore the possibility of rain. It could, you know, couldn't it? Sometimes I think they ignore the proprieties also. I jolly well wouldn't feel properly dressed, my dear, without at least a parasol."

Though I looked to other customers for vicarious excitement and real humor, I looked to Jacqueline Bouvier for companionship and a sharing of interests. There were so many things we found to share and laugh about, besides a mutual interest in fashion.

For example, we found that both of us had been bound up in pigtails—protestingly—in our school days. Suddenly an old hurt vanished and I became unashamedly amused as I told her how I'd gotten rid of mine by simply slashing them off as soon as I'd arrived at college.

"Just as I finished hacking off most of my hair, a phone call came from my minister father, saying he and Mother were coming to take me out to dinner," I recalled. "I was scared to death for I had been warned not to cut off my hair or I would be looked upon as a 'bad woman.' I tried to solve my dilemma by telling the folks that I had just washed my hair and, as it wasn't completely dry, I had tied a scarf around my head. Since I never wore a scarf like that it was a little hard for them to believe, and before my father's righteous gaze I finally broke down and confessed. I'm sure he never liked my hair short, but at least he had to revise his definition of a 'bad woman.' I never let my hair grow long again."

Just as I had once appropriated my mother's material, meant for my sister, to make a dress for myself, Jacqueline had appropriated a blanket, meant for another horse, for her horse "Danseuse." Her horse *needed* it.

Jackie seemed to fit into many worlds: the world of little children—she'd have made a crackerjack teacher—and the world of society and the world of animals, especially horses and dogs.

Jackie certainly fitted into the fashion world, too, and once I had tried to urge her to go into that world, even though she had turned down the *Vogue Prix de Paris*. "I think you would have a great future in fashion designing," I told her as I studied some of her designs.

"I want to do something useful," she said, "but I'm not sure yet what. Not that clothes aren't important, but a career like that would be limiting to me. I'm exploring another idea."

I wondered what.

From her mother I knew that Jackie was versed in many things—languages, history, art and the writing of prose and poetry. As a child, she had expressed herself almost as easily in rhymed as in unrhymed words. Government or diplomacy would have been two of many doors open to her, I felt.

I always thought that Jacqueline had reached her decision not to enter the fashion field for another, unvoiced, reason—she hated to tell other people what to do. I noticed over and over again that, while she was always very sure of what she wanted for herself, she was very careful never to impose her opinion on others. Even those who asked her for advice on clothes found it hard to get a direct answer.

One day, soon after the new year had arrived, Jackie

came flying in with a big camera slung over one shoulder and a shoulder bag over the other. She was bubbling with delight. "I have a job," she said. "I'm the Inquiring Photographer for the *Times-Herald!*"

I could hardly believe my ears. She was starting a career on a newspaper. Here again, I felt suddenly closer to her because my first job, too, had been as a reporter.

"Congratulations," I said. I went to get the paper lying on my table and looked at the column. "Why is 'photographer' spelled wrong?" I asked. "It's spelled 'photografer' here."

Jackie explained that the *Times-Herald* was campaigning to get people to spell words the way they sounded.

"And why don't I see your by-line?" I continued.

"It will come," she said. "It will come."

"Well, that shouldn't take long. You have just gained another reader."

Naturally, Jacqueline's column became my "must" reading every day, and it gave me great insight into her character, her wonderful warmth and sympathy toward people (and dogs which she also "interviewed") and what I enjoyed most, her impish sense of humor.

I felt almost more intense than she did about her getting a by-line. It was remarkable to me that a young woman, who had mingled only with society, had chosen to attempt to make her way in the workaday world—to succeed on her own merits if possible. And it was also remarkable that she, who was basically shy, developed the courage to stop strangers of every age and walk of life on the street, how she understood their interests, and was able to blend seriousness with comedy.

Now and then, when she was questioning people in Georgetown—or even in my shop—I noticed that she never talked down to them. And if they ever seemed curious about her and asked questions, she never let on

As a camera girl, Jackie's favorite subjects
were children — and her favorite outfits were
shirtwaist dresses which she could step into.
She made them interesting by alternating plaids,
checks and solid colors. Her shoulder bag
bulged with etceteras. These days she
still likes plaids — for suits.

that she had been the "Debutante of the Year" or that she had studied at the Sorbonne or that she had won an important prize. She never traded on her name or position, referring to herself only as "the inquiring photographer." She tried not to give her name at all.

When would she get a by-line? I asked again.

She was quite willing, as she explained to me, to prove herself in the age-old newspaper tradition and wait for a by-line until she merited it.

I wondered what it took to merit a by-line.

In one column she asked Jimmy Stewart, the movie star, what his secret ambition was, and he confessed that in his secret heart he'd always wanted to be a clown. I thought that merited a by-line.

Another day she had asked men if they were more interested in sports or politics, and I definitely felt what she found merited a by-line. The consensus was that even in the nation's capital they were more interested in sports. I was certainly most surprised.

I really had to laugh aloud when Jacqueline asked a group of men what kind of clothes they thought women looked best in. My favorite answer came from Barnee, the famous Washington orchestra leader who presided at the Shoreham. He insisted that women should wear green dresses with full skirts and he added, "The more frills and fluffs you can put on a dress the better. And I think women should have long hair."

I always got a lift from reading her column, by-line or no by-line. And to show what a small world this is, there was one no-by-lined column in which she asked a woman what she thought of stag parties. The woman, Mrs. Robert S. Tarnay, replied that she thought they were great, "but that's because my husband doesn't go to them." This particular husband later became my lawyer.

But getting back to her column of secret ambitions.

After that appeared, I asked Jackie what her secret ambition had been.

"To be a ballet dancer," she said.

"That's funny," I said. "So was mine."

"I did a solo to *Golliwog Cakewalk*," said Jackie.

"My solo was *Dance of the Sugarplum Fairy* from Tchaikovsky's *Nutcracker Suite.*"

We looked at each other, laughing. What more could be said?

CHAPTER 4

I AM INTERVIEWED BY THE
INQUIRING PHOTOGRAFER

I SUPPOSE it was bound to happen.

Jackie came swooping in one fine spring day, strung with shoulder bag and camera and wearing a most devilish smile. "I've come to interview you," she said. "I want to ask you a question."

"Oh no," I groaned. It was my usual negative response. "Don't ask me any questions. I'm on your side of the fence. Remember, I'm used to asking questions, not giving the answers."

"Well, today is different. It's your turn."

"I'm just a 'little dressmaker.' Who cares what I think?"

"People are just as interested in what you have to say as what anyone else says. All I want to know is, what are you giving up for Lent?"

"Oh no," I groaned again. "I will really look ridiculous if I tell the truth. Why don't you get someone else to answer that?"

"I already did," she answered, "but I want you in the column, too."

"I just hate to talk about it. Tell me what someone else said. I just don't think I can measure up."

"I don't think your competition is that terrible," she said. "Here is one of my interviews—with Janet Auchincloss, aged six."

I had to laugh. Janet, of course, was Jackie's little half-sister. When she had been born, Jackie, then about fifteen, had written a poem predicting that Janet would be the first woman President!

"Okay, let me hear what Janet is giving up for Lent."

"Well," said Jackie, "it says here, 'I'll give up fighting with my brother James. I slap him really hard sometimes when he won't sit still at TV and keeps jumping up and down in front of Howdy Doody. And then he bawls. But he better stop tormenting my dolls and grabbing them out of the chair and throwing them on the floor or I won't be able to give up slapping him for long.' "

When I heard *that*, I wasn't even sure that Jackie was serious. How can you do a column about children's comments? I wondered. But Jackie went ahead in a businesslike way and took my picture before I'd realized what she was doing.

A few days later, on Wednesday, March 26, 1952, there on page 19 of the Washington *Times-Herald*—which is now a part of *The Washington Post*—was my picture, along with Janet's. I was looking thoroughly befuddled. I'm ashamed every time I look at it. Sure enough, she put in, too, that I was a dressmaker and gave my address wrong as the 3500 block of T Street, North West. But that was close enough since it was 1820 35th Street, just off T. Unfortunately, she didn't try to improve my quote. It sounded just like me and I groaned as I read:

"I suppose I should give up sweets. I started to cut them

out in the beginning of Lent but then I stopped. It makes me mad to think I broke it when I really didn't want a piece of candy much. It wasn't even good candy. Now it seems pointless to give it up again, but I think I'll pull myself together for one more try."

The funny thing, though, was that just talking about it made me really give up candy, and I've hardly touched it since.

When next I saw Jackie I said, "Well, I don't see a by-line yet. I only hope my comments haven't prejudiced your editor against you forever."

"It will come," she said confidently, as before. "It will come."

Actually I never doubted for a minute that it would.

Jackie walked as if she knew where she were going. To me, walking, more than anything else, expresses one's true personality. If people have a lackadaisical way of moving, you know they have no ambition. In hiring assistants I judge them largely by the way they walk. I would have hired Jackie any time. She held her shoulders back and her head high. It all added up to a forthright and capable personality. She was very positive in what she was trying to do and positive in her way of expressing it. She didn't hesitate. You've seen people who make sketches that are unsure and vague. Hers were bold and positive strokes. Even the squiggles were positive.

Jackie did a lot of "walking" to get a by-line.

She was all over the map. She attended a spelling bee. (The hardest word was "chrysanthemum," which was later to be the name of my new dog.) She went to the Folger Shakespearean Library to find out which of the master's words were still applicable to today's world. One person said, "I don't even have to stop to think. It is, 'Lord, what fools these mortals be.'"

A few days after she interviewed me, she was asking

members of the male species, "When did you discover that women are *not* the weaker sex?"

Then again, she asked people how they felt about federal income taxes and what they would do with the money if they didn't have to hand it over to the Government.

And then it happened—her first by-line! March 26, 1952, was the date. She had asked people if they had any special superstitions. One person, who said he kept watching for the number of crows he saw in one flock, recited a little rhyme I couldn't get out of my head:

> One crow, sorrow
> Two crows, joy
> Three crows, a wedding
> Four crows, a boy.

The next time I saw Jacqueline I congratulated her that the crows had finally done the trick.

I told her, "Your column is very educational."

"I'm glad of that, Mrs. Rhea," she said with mock seriousness.

"Well, I'm not," I retorted. "I don't have time to look for crows out of the window and I find myself repeating the jingle to the rhythm of my sewing. It's driving me crazy."

"I'll work up one for the sewing machine rhythm," she laughed.

"Thanks."

Jackie's second by-lined column was a corker, too. She asked a bunch of average men right around my neighborhood in Georgetown what they thought of psychoanalysis. I loved one of the answers, and I could just imagine Jacqueline putting it down verbatim, tongue in cheek. "Psychoanalysis is not natively American," this particular man said bitterly. "It was brought in by foreigners and has never added one bit to this country's peace of mind."

Looking back, how carefree was that spring of 1952, how relaxed and happy-go-lucky! Children bounding in and out on their way to school. Customers talking and laughing. Me swapping anecdotes about my children with mothers like Mrs. Auchincloss, who could top me with the stories of their offspring. Jackie shopping a lot in the New York stores—Lord and Taylor, Bonwit's, Sak's Fifth Avenue and Bergdorf's—and having the dresses sent directly to me so that I could go to work on them, since I had the muslin pattern of her figure and had met with her approval by using my "magic dart." She was a little long-waisted and sometimes the waistline needed adjustment too.

Jackie would arrive, ring the bell and let herself in, very casually. More often than not, I would be downstairs in the workroom, busy at my sewing machine.

When I'd hear her quick little rings, I'd hurry upstairs. Jackie would be half undressed for her fitting by the time I came into the fitting room, my arms draped with her dresses. Other customers were often late. Other customers would have a million excuses for why they couldn't make it on time—the maid hadn't arrived, the dog was sick, and even once, "there was an escaped monkey trying to get into my window!"

But Jackie, with the best excuse in the world—because she was always on assignment for her paper and could have pleaded that a special interview delayed her—never used an excuse and was never late. If she were only sixty seconds late she would say, "I'm terribly sorry, Mrs. Rhea."

"Oh Jackie, you're not late at all. You have nothing to apologize for."

I used to tell Margy, "If everyone were like Jackie, the world would go around smoother."

Jackie would phone early in the morning to make her appointment. She would say, "Mrs. Rhea," (she always called me that, while everyone else called me *Miss* Rhea)

"I wonder if you'd be able to see me this afternoon about two or three. I have to be out your way anyway."

I always had many appointments with the women in her circle at that time of the day, and the career women came in after their office hours, around five o'clock. But I would always try to oblige Jacqueline, making the appointment as close as possible to the hour she wished. "Well, I already have a 2:00 and a 3:00 o'clock appointment," I might answer, "but you're so easy to fit that I think I can squeeze you in at 2:40."

"That will be t-rrific. I'll be there."

And she was.

She'd get out of her little black convertible, noticing every little thing as she came to my white picket fence and up the steps. "Your dogwood's in bloom," she said one day. "Do you know?"

I didn't and I went to the window to look at that tiny pathetic little tree that had been trying to produce just one little flower in overcrowded Georgetown.

"Well, that's a surprise! I really thought it would never make it." I looked at what appeared to me a miracle on that smallest of all dogwoods. There were three—no less—white buds, and one had actually opened.

My house was one of four flat-front attached houses. Mine was on the end, and next to it, on the left as you came up the walk, was a vacant lot. In the lot was a huge, luxurious tree, flourishing on neglect. My dogwood had sat in the middle of my postage stamp front yard and lapped up all the care I lavished on it, with no noticeable gratitude until this day.

As I looked at the tree with its fledgling blossoms, I noticed a bunch of children already clustered around Jackie's car. "Gordon Junior High is waiting for you," I informed her. "Jimi will be home in a minute."

Jimi went to Gordon Junior High across the street and

Sylvia to Western High which was a block down. It had not taken long for the Gordon children to spread the word that the girl with the camera was THE girl who could get their picture in the paper.

Every morning my house was the rallying point for the girls of the neighborhood on their way to school. First came the gang to pick up Sylvia and they would check themselves in my big mirror. They would put on their make-up, check their slips, straighten their stocking seams and re-comb their hair and then saunter out the door, as sophisticated as women of the world going to a cocktail party. You may be sure that they gave the display dress on my fitting room form a careful once-over and, in leaving, often graciously assured me that it was "stunning, simply stunning." I would hide a smile and start to pick up the loose hair they had dropped on the carpet.

They would hardly be out of the house when the second batch arrived—Jimi's friends. They would stand gangling before the mirror, making faces at themselves and each other, pretending they couldn't care less about how they looked. But they looked, anyhow.

I had to shoo them out before my first customer arrived and so they wouldn't be late to school. Sometimes the first customer would be coming up the stairs as they were jumping down and she would say, "Which one is yours, Miss Rhea?"

"The loudest."

Sometimes, when Jackie was there in the afternoon, she would watch with amusement as I tried to shoo a bevy of girls away from the telephone. They had a habit of using my phone to call their homes with a million and one questions and details on where they were spending the afternoon, and how to reach them in case of such and such an "emergency." You couldn't fence those kids out.

"You're an indulgent mother," said Jackie.

"You wouldn't get my daughters to agree with you."
I was thinking of the times I had tried to enforce my rule
about keeping out of the living room when a fitting began.
They were especially rebellious when Jackie was there
because her career fascinated them more than had her contest winning or her fashion designing. They wanted to peep
at the Inquiring Photographer—whose column, incidentally, was re-named "The Inquiring Camera Girl." They
wanted to know what she was wearing, because they both
fully intended to try for her career some day.

As for Jackie, she was playing the role of girl reporter
with relish and dressing the part. Neat, black, dressmaker
suits were the order of the day. Neat white shirt collar
folded out over the jacket. I made several of these suits.
Some came from the store racks in New York.

One of her favorite girl-reporter outfits was a gray
pleated skirt and black turtle-neck sweater with a wide
black belt. She also liked to use a wide belt, of darker
color, on several light-colored print dresses, thinking this
made her waist look slimmer. She was very waist-conscious
in those days.

The sleeves were almost invariably three-quarter length,
going against the almost universal rule at that time. Everyone else her age, who came to me, wanted either long
sleeves or short ones high above the elbow.

I have the copy of *Vogue* published at the time she and
the other contest winners were announced. The photographs of the four show that two of the girls had long
sleeves and the third had short ones. Only Jacqueline wore
the more unusual three-quarter length.

Jackie designed, at this time, several dresses that would
be easy to step into. "I can't be bothered with complications," she said. Some of the step-in dresses were shirtwaist
ones. As I recall, she wore shirtwaist dresses before they became so standard. She started wearing them for work and a

One of Jackie's pet career girl costumes
consisted of a black turtle neck sweater and
plaid skirt. She never wore extremely high
heels for work or dress-up — always pumps

few years later they practically became a must for every career girl. Jackie gave them a little dash by wearing them in bold plaids or checks.

Her shoes were black low-heeled pumps to match the inevitable leather shoulder-strap bag into which she poured flash bulbs, pencils, notebooks, make-up, gloves, magazines, swatches of cloth, bric-a-brac, incidentals and what have you. That bulging "badge of the girl reporter" seemed to delight Jacqueline.

How well she looked the part of the "average" girl intent on her career was brought home to me forcefully one day by the husband of one of my customers who came to call for his wife and saw Jackie as she was leaving.

"You know," he said, "if that girl with the camera is a commercial photographer, she could pick up some extra money. I've been needing to have some pictures taken down at the office. You can suggest it to her, if you like."

I had to explain that I didn't think that Jackie would be interested in "picking up some extra money." He looked disappointed as he left.

Jackie, though she had no money worries, did know the value of money. She never dickered about prices, but she almost always asked in advance what something would cost. In buying clothes at stores she was not extravagant but got good value for value received.

What I would have liked to have told the man, but didn't, was that Jackie could hardly afford *me* on her salary. My dresses started at $35 and went up to $100 and beyond. Jackie's starting salary on the *Times-Herald* was $42.50 a week.

◄❧CHAPTER 5❧►

A VERY BRIEF ENCOUNTER

WITH HER BY-LINE safely attached to her column, Jackie was off and running. To make her work stand out, she gave the column the same full attention she had given the *Vogue* contest, and as far as I could see it had, by April of '52, already become a conversation piece. All my customers were discussing it. Many, who didn't know her or the fact that she was also a customer of mine, would mention a Jacqueline column they had read and quote some humorous question or answer.

Some were proud that a girl was doing so well. A few, who knew her wealthy background, complained that she was taking the job away from some man who needed it, and others, I suspected, were jealous. But for the most part, even her wealthy friends gave her credit for steering away from the easy life she could have with its round of pleasant parties and no exertion.

Jackie's luck was evident when, just two months after she had her first by-line, she rated a special mention in print from her editor. The Nats, the Washington baseball team, had been taking a beating and Jackie went out to Griffith Stadium and interviewed the men just before their game with the Athletics.

I could just imagine the scene where Jackie arrived at the stadium and flabbergasted the big huskies by asking them, point blank, if they were ready to "pull out" of their slump.

How could they say "No" to this beautiful creature?

The editor's note above her column that historic May 27, 1952, said: "Jacqueline seems to have been what our ball club needed. A short time after she sweetly asked the Nats when they were going to start slugging again, the club exploded with 13 hits and defeated the Athletics 5 to 3. Ed."

I told Jackie I bet the editor was glad now that he had given her the job!

I was interested to learn that the man who had been the "Inquiring Photografer" before her was a student who had worked his way through college to become a physician. He is the one who helped Jackie learn the ropes: how to pick interesting-looking people and how to stop them with some provocative question. Jackie learned quickly.

"What didn't you give up after you got married?" was one of her questions to appear in her *Times-Herald* column, and it certainly started some interesting discussions in my fitting room.

So did the one in which my customers and I learned that the feminine ancestor of a D.A.R., whom Jackie interviewed on the subject of genealogy, had singlehandedly scalped twelve Indians after they killed her baby.

And, "What do you think of wrestling as a sport for women?"

And, "Are wives a luxury or a necessity?"

And, "Do you think a wife should tell her husband that he's smarter than she?"

And, "If you could have three wishes, what would they be?" My daughters wished they could grow up to look like Jackie and be inquiring camera girls.

I noticed that Jackie wasted no opportunity to combine business and pleasure, which showed that she already knew the old newspaper trick of making the most of life.

For example, going to Middleburg for the hunter trials, she tossed off a column on "What do you like best about fox hunting?"

I don't know why Jackie was at the veterinary's—it probably had something to do with one of the dogs at the Auchincloss home—but the column that resulted from her visit to the small animal hospital in Georgetown, run by Dr. Jean S. Goudy—who, incidentally, still practices there—became my favorite of all her columns, and I clipped it to add to my growing "Jackie" collection.

It was, if you really want to know, simply an interview with dogs, in which Jackie was asking each dog what it was doing at the vet's. I laughed till I cried as the dogs told her, without hesitation, what was going on and they had no false modesty about giving their names, ages and pedigrees. But the first dog made me sad.

That was Trudle, aged five, who was there with a psychological problem. "I'm in the maternity ward. I just had five puppies." (One for every year of her age.) But she confided that now, when she should have been happiest, she was miserable. "They took my puppies away because they weren't pure dachshunds." She told Jackie, "I can't eat. I just want my puppies back."

Then there was a stout-hearted gentleman boxer, age seven, who said, "What am I doing here? My dear Lady, I ask myself the same question." A little later he admitted that he did have a slight "corneal ulcer—nothing serious."

There was Cracker, a cocker spaniel, who said he'd gone "to Florida for my health and ended up by losing it completely." He'd developed a little case of asthma and a touch of intestinal infection from a garbage can, and on top of it all the climate had "simply wrecked" his nerves.

Another cocker, thirteen-year-old Simon, told Jackie, "I'm an old man." But he added, philosophically, "I'm resigned to spending most of my time in doctors' offices these days."

Sis, a miniature schnauzer, said she "couldn't be more annoyed" about being at the vet's. She had simply taken a bite out of a nurse whom she couldn't stand. "I bit her good and hard," she said, "and I was dumped here to board till my owner recovers. And that better be soon, I'm telling you."

Only one cat made the column, a Persian named Zenda, who spoke for her husband and herself. She told how the family had gone South without them because of a silly rule barring cats from hotels. "We could use a vacation too," said Zenda, "and as for hotels not letting us in, we're far better than dogs."

When Jackie came in after that I said, "Your column shows you certainly know how to bring out the best in man or beast."

"But I seem to bring out the worst in little children," she laughed. "You should hear some of their frank answers."

"I read one," I said, and went to get the column in which a little girl had told what she thought of little boys—in rhyme, yet. "Grunty old goldfish and tattletale ginger-ale, stick your hand in the garbage pail."

"Yes," she said, "and that isn't the worst of it. How about where she tells how Donald kicked Edmund's tooth out and he bled all over the place?"

"Yes," I agreed. "Perfect little ladies and gentlemen all the way."

Jackie was wearing her favorite sweater and belted skirt working-costume and carrying over her arm a suit of heavy faille. "I got this suit in France, but I wonder if you can do something with the jacket. I feel just like a penguin every time I wear it."

I examined the suit. "It's beautiful, simply beautiful."

"Isn't it?" she said. "But the front is cut too deep for me. I realize that now."

"Well, let's see what can be done," I said.

The skirt had a slim straight look. The jacket was fitted at the waist with a double-breasted effect. But the item which was bothering Jackie was the collar which swooped down below the bustline in a curve, making quite a deep opening, so that the white blouse was prominently displayed—just like a man's full dress shirt or, as Jackie had said, the snowy white front of an Emperor penguin.

Creative alteration, as I called it, had been my specialty since I opened my own business in 1947. That was the year of the "new look" when Dior had created a furor and caused anguished wails because he decreed that dresses, which had been knee-length since the war, should drop to very near the ankle. Everyone had been caught off guard.

Drawing on every trick I could think of, including some I had learned in childhood when working on my doll dresses, I tried to rescue dresses and suits—some of them brand-new—which were suddenly as outdated as a dodo.

Many new customers came to me because they read about me in *The Washington Daily News.* "Put the name Mini Rhea on your memo pad," it advised women, because she can "make dresses from pictures and doesn't require patterns" and she "knows all kinds of tricks to give last year's suits, coats and dresses this year's new long look."

"Why don't you slip into that suit and let me see why

. . but this is the suit Jackie did not
like after she brought it from France.
She didn't like long sleeves and she said of
the deep-cut front, "It makes me look like
a penguin." She gave it to me because I looked
well in it

you think you look like a penguin in it," I suggested. I noticed the suit had full-length sleeves and I was sure this had helped prejudice her against it.

Jackie backed off to scrutinize me, cocking her head and looking me up and down. "I have a better idea," she said at last. "Why don't you try it on, Mrs. Rhea? It wouldn't look like that on you."

I did.

She was right—I did *not* look like a penguin in it. I got so many compliments on it, because it increased my stature and lengthened my short neck, that when the skirt wore out I made a new one to go with the jacket. The First Lady would be surprised to learn that I still have the suit and wear it often, although it has seen almost a decade of hard wear.

I wondered if Jackie knew how lucky she was. She had no bad figure faults—no short neck, as I had—no physical defects that needed to be camouflaged, no short stature or short legs that plague some women who are lovely in all other respects.

I had one customer, with an envied social position, who had a scar in the center of her back, and in making evening clothes we devised special effects that would sweep artfully across that particular spot.

Another had one shoulder higher than the other. By building up one shoulder with unseen padding and other eye-fooling tricks in high-necked dresses, and by using slanting lines and covering only one shoulder in evening gowns, no one could ever detect this defect.

But I had many customers with lovely, flawless figures. The three ladies of the Auchincloss household were prime examples.

Jackie's mother and sister had lovely figures, which were quite alike. Both were shorter and more rounded than Jackie, with smaller waists and fuller bosoms. Lee definitely took after her mother. Jackie brought Lee to introduce her and have me do some work for her, and I immediately noticed the difference in the taste of the two sisters. I remember Jackie saying, "Don't try to make us look alike."

Where Jackie liked more inconspicuous clothes, Lee preferred the more extreme styles and more striking colors. Lee also went in for costumes with sharp color contrasts, like black and white. She liked vivid colors, like bright green and sharp yellow, which Jackie would not wear in those days. Lee wore purple when it was rarely worn. She loved red too.

I recall one outfit which Lee had in which the lining of the jacket and the dress it was made for were both black. The jacket was white and the effect of the contrast of black and white was heightened by the fact that the jacket came to two points at the neck opening and rolled back in triangular revers.

Lee loved hats, particularly dramatic ones, while Jackie wore no hats in those days. And Lee liked patterned materials much more than Jackie did.

To show how women do not change their basic taste in clothes, the other day I saw a photograph of Lee—now Princess Radziwill—in a two-piece outfit in which the flowered cloth hat matched the material of the blouse she was wearing, and a drape of material from the hat swept across the neck to produce a dramatically feminine picture.

Mrs. Auchincloss was as fond of brown as Jackie was of black and, using it as her basic color, geared much of her wardrobe to it. She never wore tight sheaths—always a soft, full skirt. Her necklines were either a deep scoop or square. She did not care for the higher necklines which Jackie wore.

Mrs. Auchincloss was easy to fit. I remember having trouble on only one dress which I made for her. It was a heavy brown velvet—a long formal gown with a short jacket. It was very conservative and elegant, with a low square neck and black ornamentation. It just wouldn't drape right. But eventually I straightened it out. I must say Mrs. Auchincloss was more than patient. She was sympathetic.

Sometimes she brought James, and also Janet, who was named for her. She lived such a busy life that she came only in the morning or late in the afternoon. She was always on the go—just like Jacqueline.

Mrs. Auchincloss was so dainty and petite that I was surprised to learn that she was an accomplished sportswoman. Both Jackie and her mother had won ribbons in horse shows, separately and as a mother-daughter team. Mrs. Auchincloss was understandably proud that Jackie won her first ribbon for riding at the age of eleven.

But Jackie, I was told, had been in the public eye since she was two. On her second birthday party she made the society columns as an outstanding little hostess who provided ponies for her guests to ride, and again that year she was written up as a dog fancier—she had exhibited her Scotch terrier, "Hoochie," at a dog show in which her Grandmother Bouvier also had an entry.

I wondered how Mrs. Auchincloss was taking the fact that her daughter was now *writing* news instead of *making* it. From what she said, it was clear that Jackie's mother would back her loyally in any career she chose, but I also had the impression that she didn't think Jackie's newspaper phase would last forever.

"It's excellent experience for Jackie," said Mrs. Auchincloss. "But I'm just as curious to see what she does next as you are," and she laughed as if she indeed enjoyed standing on the side lines and watching, but never interfering in the development of her talented daughter.

Jackie was not my only customer from the Fourth Estate.

I used to reflect that I had enough girl reporters to put out my own newspaper. My most famous writing client was Ruth Montgomery, the fashionable King Features Syndicate writer, known for her astoundingly blue eyes as well as for her sharp, incisive wit, which she used effectively in her column to cut high Government officials and social leaders down to size.

Ruth was one of my favorite and most attractive customers. She was also a close neighbor. Since she had a hectic schedule to keep, I often fitted her into my early morning hours so she could be free to go about her interviews. What always impressed me was how she could be such a complete career woman and still maintain her femininity.

The society and women's page writers of the *Times-Herald* accounted for more than one customer. *The Washington Post* and *The Washington Daily News* were also represented in my guest book. Some of the feminine reporters were on periodicals such as *U.S. News and World Report,* and some of the women wrote straight news stories for the wire services, while others were in television and radio.

But not all the newscasters and writers on my customer list were female.

Scripps-Howard columnist Don Hearn used to wear my sport shirts. Commentator Jerry Strong, whose wife, Jimma, was one of my pet customers, had me make him a riding jacket out of some beautiful Italian silk that had been brought to him from abroad. One of the oddest things I ever made was for a sentimental newspaperman who wanted to remember the places he'd been by the ties he wore there. He talked me into ripping them up and making a patchwork jacket out of them! Needless to say, this was a job that I would not like to repeat, but it did turn out very well.

Then there were the wives and daughters of famous

newspapermen. Mrs. Elmer Davis and her daughter, Anne, introduced me to the wonders of a beautiful hand-woven material crafted in North Carolina. It was absolutely indestructible. Her husband flew around the word wearing a suit of this material, the only suit he took along on his assignment. When he arrived back home it looked as fresh as when he had left. Mrs. Davis mentioned that F.D.R. had most of his suits made of this cloth.

Through Mrs. Walter Lippmann, I got mentioned in her husband's column. She had come back from Paris with a suit that had been made there, and it was not a good fit. It was impossible to alter it satisfactorily. She was so disappointed that she had me make another suit to take its place. One day Walter Lippman took note of the incident in his column to say that it was a shame people didn't know we had just as good dressmakers here as abroad. What he didn't know was that I, too, had come under the influence of French designers now that I was studying their work in French fashion magazines under Jacqueline's tutelage.

During the fittings for Mrs. Lippmann I learned from her as much about the world of travel as I did about the fashion world from Jacqueline.

Mrs. Auchincloss' friend, Mrs. Arthur Krock, was a most lovely and gracious customer. I shall always be grateful to her for many things. She influenced, not only my life, but Jacqueline's too, in a roundabout way.

It was her husband, a Washington correspondent for *The New York Times,* who called the editor of the *Times-Herald* and arranged for Jacqueline to be interviewed for a position. But after that, Jackie was on her own, having to win the job on her own merits.

From various customers of the newspaper world I heard that Jacqueline was very well liked at the *Times-Herald* and respected for her "guts" in taking a job in a field where she had had no previous training. The reporters and photographers, young and old, volunteered their services in helping the fledgling. I heard that one photographer, in a burst of enthusiasm, became a human tape measure to show Jackie exactly how far away her subject should be when she snapped the shutter.

"You should be just six feet away. I'm exactly six feet tall. Look!" And so saying, he lay prone upon the floor, so she could get the feel of six feet. I'm sure Jackie will never forget *that* newspaperman.

Jackie developed her film on the fourth floor of the old *Times-Herald* building at 13th and H Streets. Then she would go to the fifth floor to use someone's typewriter to write her column.

I heard how many of the reporters and photographers would gang up to kid her at the office. They would say, "What's a beautiful girl like you doing messing around with the hypo?" (They were referring to the chemical used in developing photographs.) Jackie would ask them sweetly why they weren't doing it for her.

"We're all thinking of taking a powder and going out to your pool this afternoon, how about it?" they'd tease.

"T-rrific," she'd answer.

But when the men on the *Times-Herald* would ask her out, she was very gentle in the way she let them down. "I'm going out with a group of friends," she'd say. She never accepted a date from any of her co-workers. When they'd ask her, she'd always be so sorry but all tied up. One of the photographers, Frank Mahaney, would help protect her from the "4th Floor Wolves," as they were called.

When the going got too tough around the *Times-Herald,* Jackie would escape to the *International News Service,* Washington Bureau, which was on the sixth floor of the *Times-Herald* building, where she would sit and chat awhile with re-write man James Lee, who had been a well-known Hollywood writer before coming to Washington, and William K. Hutchinson, the INS Washington

Bureau Chief, known for his toughness and fiery tongue.

For some reason, Hutch, a bachelor, was mild and even gentle with Jackie. He seemed to be especially intrigued by the keen mind of this inquiring reporter. And once he did a bit of inquiring himself, concerning the inquiring photographer's costume. She was wearing a simple black dress, the only ornamentation of which was some gold lettering on a black belt.

He looked at it curiously. "What does that say?"

Jackie rattled off the famous French phrase, "Honi soit qui mal y pense." ("Evil to him who evil thinks.")

Jackie could see the tough newspaperman knew nothing about French. "It means, 'Love me, love my dog,' " she said.

"Oh," he said, seriously, not realizing she was pulling his leg. And not a soul in the office told Hutch what the lettering on the belt really meant.

Then, happy with her joke, she took the elevator back down to the fifth floor to face her *Times-Herald* gang of tormentors, waiting to plague her for a date. "Why don't you date reporters, Jackie? What's wrong with us?"

However, there was a reporter she had dated in the past who was the second newspaperman to influence her life, Arthur Krock being the first. The second was Charles Bartlett of the *Chattanooga Times,* who arranged a dinner party at his home in Georgetown so that she could meet a certain bachelor Congressman.

To Bartlett's delight, the brief encounter seemed to presage a budding romance. But when the Congressman escorted Jackie to her car and suggested they go some place, he found a large masculine figure looming in the back seat.

Jackie recovered quickly and made the introductions.

It was an old boy friend who happened to see her car and decided to surprise her. But it was too much surprise for the Congressman, who quickly excused himself and left.

The Congressman's name was John Fitzgerald Kennedy.

--→《CHAPTER 6》→--

LESSONS FROM THE FRENCH

I DON'T RECALL exactly when I realized it, but somewhere along the way during that summer of 1952 I knew that Jacqueline had started dating the Congressman.

I have read that after the fiasco of their first meeting; it had taken something like seven months for them to get together again. Jackie had left to tour Europe with Lee and it was not until Jackie became engaged and then had broken off with Husted that I realized the man called "Washington's most eligible bachelor" was in the picture.

After Husted and Jackie were no longer seeing each other, his aunt, Mrs. Husted, and her three daughters who were also my customers, would still run into Jackie at my shop and they were as good friends as ever. I would hear them talk about the swimming pool and Jackie would invite them all to come out and cool off.

Jackie herself would first have to work in the broiling sun getting her even half-dozen subjects before she could join them at the poolside.

But Jackie could always use her wits to good advantage

in order to be where things were more comfortable and pleasant. I remember one hot July day that found her at the cooler tree-lined Haines Point links asking, "What makes you maddest on the golf course?"

And another hot day she toured the "hot spots" asking, "How do you keep cool?"

Then, still beating the weather, she interviewed some men idly fishing on the shady bank of the Potomac River near Chain Bridge, inquiring, "What is the biggest fish story you ever told or heard?"

The Republican nomination came and went without a ripple. Jackie bothered with only one political question: "What do you think of General Eisenhower winning the nomination on the first ballot?"

I asked her if she was going to take a greater interest in the campaign and she said she felt she'd leave politics to the political writers and stick to human interest.

Jackie really did have a way of provoking people to thought. Once she asked, "What prominent person's death affected you most?" and even some of my most rock-ribbed Republican customers confessed how they had cried and been inconsolable at the death of President Roosevelt, feeling, suddenly, that he had done his best, though "misguided," and, in effect, had given his life for his country.

She asked whether juvenile delinquents should have their fingerprints sent to the FBI like those of hardened criminals, and another stimulating question was, "What was the most difficult decision you ever had to make?"

She almost caused a fight between two top Government secretaries, who came for a fitting together, after she asked in her *Times-Herald* column, "Do you think you understand your boss better than his wife does?" One of the women was sure she did and this, for some unknown reason, caused most righteous indignation in the other.

Another rumpus in my dressing room was stirred up by

the question, "Do you consider yourself normal?" And when her column on "Do you often change your impression of people?" appeared, I learned that many women blamed their marital problems and practically every other problem on the fact that when they met someone they assumed he was as he seemed to be, and refused to change their minds until they had "been burned." It was a sorry fact that most women went by first impressions.

In thinking back over her columns, however, the one question she asked at that time which applied most to herself—though she'd have been surprised to know it—was, "Do you think your life story would make a good movie?" Only in retrospect can I see that she, herself, was right then living the making of a good movie story, complete with two handsome men—John Fitzgerald Kennedy and Henry Cabot Lodge—fighting for a great and desired position, a seat in the Senate. Her hero was the dark horse candidate.

But talk about absentee romances! She was in one again. She had broken her engagement with Husted, saying it was "too much long distance." Now she was waiting for phone calls, waiting for news, waiting for the Congressman's short visits between his hurried trips to Massachusetts to speak or attend brunches in every hamlet and four corners.

"This is a romance?" I thought.

But Jackie proved she had absorbed not only French fashion styles but the French woman's serenity and ability to wait. And not only to wait, but to wait sweetly and contentedly. Oh, what I would give for this trait! And she exuded happiness. I found this a wonderful opportunity, when Jackie was killing a little time, to pore over the French fashion magazines with her.

I cannot stress too much how important these magazines were in changing my fashion approach and outlook. I now studied the clothes of my French and other foreign customers of the diplomatic world with new interest and appreciation.

It seemed to me that Jackie was definitely oriented toward the French. She liked the language, the literature and the fashions. She spoke of things French with affection and said, laughingly, "Well, after all, the Bouviers are French."

The first Bouvier who came to America, inspired by Lafayette's passion for freedom, helped fight the British at Yorktown. But he had gone back to Grenoble, the family home. His son returned to America and amassed a fortune in Philadelphia, where a street is still named for him, just a few blocks from my shop.

Incidentally, Jackie's sister, Caroline Lee, was named after Caroline Ewing, who had defied her Protestant family in Philadelphia and married a Roman Catholic, John Vernou Bouvier. This great-grandmother had been concerned with the problems of the world and she performed an untold number of acts of charity—among them, setting up the New York Foundling Hospital for unwanted children of all races and religions.

Jackie, I thought, was a lot like this great-grandmother, having depth and understanding and sympathy for the highest and the lowest. She was interested in the lives of all people and curious to fathom their inner impulses.

Jackie was self-sufficient, didn't want me to fix her hooks or help her with a zipper. Some of my customers treated me like a maid, stepping out of their clothes and leaving them on the floor for me to pick up while they watched. But Jackie didn't want a lady's maid and she had great respect for every individual.

Caroline Lee had more of the grand manner than Jackie. Lee did not talk as much or share her thoughts, or express interest in me—a little dressmaker. It wasn't that she was unkind; it was just that she did not have the special warmth that was Jacqueline's.

Lee reminded me now and then of the Duchess of Windsor—there was even a slight resemblance. I mentioned this once to Jackie as we mulled over what was doing in Paris and she merely smiled.

I had come to realize that fashion was only one facet of Jackie's personality. Fashion, as far as she was concerned, was just one more way of self-expression, like talking and painting and writing.

I used to be amazed at how much more pleasure the French—and Jackie—could get out of fashion than the Americans could. My French customers, I noticed, had fun with clothes. To a Frenchwoman, her clothes are a part of her personality and with the ever-present Gallic humor, she looks upon clothes as objects to make life more gay and amusing. Because of this, she never acts apologetic. She says about a dress, "Isn't it a joy?" and she really enjoys wearing it.

I noticed that when the French women talked to me about clothes, they acted animated and happy. When American women consulted me, they sounded a little timid and afraid of criticism and wanted reassurance about whether they "dare" wear something. They would say, "Will someone call me a clotheshorse if I wear this?"

The Frenchwoman enjoys being a clotheshorse and revels in attracting attention. The American woman goes one step forward and two steps back, coming in with a good idea—and a daring one—and then retreating when she fears she may be the only one wearing this type of dress. If I've heard it once, I've heard it a million times, "Oh, I'm afraid I'll be conspicuous. Let's add a little something here, or do something to tone down the extreme look."

The dress would become just another dress.

An American woman is intent on having a dress or suit

which no one will remember the next time she wears it. A Frenchwoman hopes you *will* remember the dress she wore before and admire it again.

As I studied the magazines, I realized that French women refuse to be tied down to rigid rules. All American shoulder seams at that time came exactly to the shoulder. No variety. But, ah! the French! A suit could have a shoulder seam halfway down the arm, or it might have a sleeve that looked like a child's drawing—cut in one piece right with the body part and no shoulder seam at all. Or it might have a yoke which would include the sleeve. That particular style which put a straight line across the top of the bust did wonders to lessen the height of a too tall woman.

The French used other tricks to make a small woman look tall and think tall—lines pointing up, up; pointed Renaissance hats, hiding all the hair; extremely straight side seams to give a woman the classic dignity of a Grecian column.

In America the flared skirt was a must and poor little short women were looking even shorter and more insignificant in them.

The French were turning a bit to the Greek for inspiration in the early Nineteen Fifties, and I was thrilled to see, not long ago, that this beautiful Grecian style was worn by the First Lady at the White House—one bare shoulder and all. It brought back memories.

I used to wish that all American girls would be taught the principles of line and design as a compulsory part of their high school education and that every housewife had at least one French fashion magazine. Then, I thought, maybe we'd stop acting like a bunch of sheep, all wearing crinolines or all wearing dresses the same prescribed number of inches above the ankle. I thought how surprised some of these girls and their mothers would be to learn, as I had, that the French don't feel they must make a shoulder line at the shoulder or a waistline at the waist or a straight hemline at the hem.

I remember once a young customer—a bride-to-be—fell in love with a picture of a suit she saw in my first French magazine and wanted one just like it for her going-away suit. It was the first extreme French style I'd copied from a picture.

Being used to the American way, I was lost without that familiar landmark of the standard shoulder seam. I tried to figure out how I could cut the material. I got more and more confused. Finally, I started draping the muslin material on the form and cut it that way. To my great surprise, I found that it was ten times simpler than anything I'd done before. The French, I found, do really cut with a free hand. The sleeves had low dropped armholes and the neckline was cut deep, with a large collar. It had a loosely fitted waist and hidden buttons. The skirt was very fitted and slim. The whole effect was of clean lines.

I once said to Jacqueline that the Frenchwoman wears her clothes, whereas the clothes wear the American woman.

American clothes seemed to look limp in comparison with the French clothes. Part of that was due to the way that American women wore their clothes. They seemed to be careless about their posture and their walk. No matter how lovely a dress is, if it is not worn with good posture, with head held high and with pride, it does nothing for a person.

Then I learned that another reason for the superior French look is that French clothes have much more body, not only in the materials used, but in the way they are made. If one has ever ripped up a French suit in order to make an alteration on it, that person will know what I mean. Under the silk lining is the muslin interfacing, that has been stitched and re-stitched, and placed over finely overcast seams, then boned in places, which makes it almost impossible to get to the original seam to re-stitch.

When I started ripping apart the first French suit brought in to me for alteration, I thought, "This will be easy because it has such simple lines." But when I had released the lining and took a good look at what was underneath I soon saw that it was as complicated on the inside as it was uncomplicated outside. This was, I realized, a good way to get a lesson in French sewing technique, so I slowed down and studied each step. In the interfacing the darts were cut away and overlapped and then stitched to eliminate the bulk. Frequently Americans just cut and press open the darts, which can leave a mark on the outside of the suit. The whole suit, I found, was lined with interfacing to give more shape to it and keep that relaxed look from being marred by wrinkles. I could picture the hours of handwork that had gone into the invisible part of the suit.

The same inside work, I soon discovered, was also in their daytime dresses, which means that French clothes can even look good on a hanger, whereas ours are apt to look limp and lifeless. Thank goodness, American manufacturers for the past few years have caught on to the fact that clothes do not necessarily have to be custom-made to be lined, but that even the medium price range of frocks can have more shape and chic with lining. But we still have quite a way to go.

Jackie insisted on dress linings and at least part of the French construction in her clothes. I remember when I made a bathing outfit for her in the summer of '52; the little white piqué jacket to go with the white halter top suit was a delight to behold, yet was guaranteed not to go limp the first time she lounged in it or drenched it in the water. The interfacing of the jacket was hidden by a flamboyant orange print that went beautifully with Jackie's dark hair and healthy suntan.

I made a lot of playtime dresses that summer for Jackie, and some career girl dresses. It was the summer she was testing out her own look of no collar, no sleeves, slightly full, gathered skirt, or skirt with big box pleats. No pockets. I would see this look grow more and more important to her and become, when she had gotten rid of the tight waist, the "Jackie look" which first intrigued the nation as they became acquainted with her through the newspapers.

The ultimate triumph of Jacqueline's fashion personality did not come about until she stopped trying to make her waist look smaller and her bust look larger and carried her straight slimness to its own final look of simplicity, making well-rounded women drool with envy that they weren't flatter and straighter-waisted.

The leadership of Jackie in the fashion world I consider to be the direct outcome of her French background and training. And so the credit should be shared by France and America.

I think the best illustration of the difference between the French look and the American look is that of a French customer who confided to me one day that she was wearing an American suit.

"It's t-rrific," I said, copying Jackie's pet phrase, which by now had become mine, too. "Wherever did you get it? It looks French somehow."

My customer laughed merrily as she pirouetted for my inspection. The front of the suit was utterly plain and unfitted. The opening of the longish jacket came in back, which was dramatic, with a big bow at the hip, and buttons.

"Utterly charming," I said. "Very original."

"Oui," she said, "it should be. Watch." So saying, she

took off the jacket, turned it around and put it on again. Suddenly it looked like every other suit. She had made the suit look French by wearing the suit backwards!

"That's how I wear all my American clothes," she said gleefully. "I fix them. Front to back. Simple."

That was the secret. Utterly simple fronts. A decoration that comes as a surprise.

That was my best lesson from the French.

CHAPTER 7

MIRROR, MIRROR ON THE— FITTING ROOM—WALL

I KNEW where Jacqueline got her warmth. It was from her mother who continued, when she came in for fittings, to head first for the phone to check on how the children were. I've heard many people talk of Mrs. Auchincloss' kindness—people from maids and matrons to a myriad others. I remember that once the hairdresser, to whom Mrs. Auchincloss and I both went at Per's in Georgetown, voiced the anxious wish that he had a car to drive on a trip he was taking to Connecticut. Mrs. Auchincloss insisted that he use her Jaguar. He was so speechless he hardly knew how to thank her, but Mrs. Auchincloss never did things for the thanks she received.

It came my turn to experience her bounty. One day she said, "Miss Rhea, could you use a larger mirror in the fitting room?"

My bank book balance flashed before my eyes and I said, "It really depends on how much you want for it."

"My goodness, I don't want anything," she said, looking a bit shocked. "I'm re-decorating my husband's den and I don't need the mirror. We'd like you to have it."

So the next day a truck arrived and the lovely huge mirror was installed on my wall. Even though I've moved several times since then that mirror has gone with me wherever I went. It is now a much-valued part of my present dressmaking establishment off Rittenhouse Square in Philadelphia, and priceless to me for its sentimental value. When I sold my shop in Washington, it was the one thing I could not part with, and though my friends thought I was crazy, I had it crated and off it went with me to Baltimore, then back to Washington and finally to Philadelphia.

Wouldn't anyone be nostalgic about a gift from a woman so kind? She stood by once to help me keep my business open. I had been ill for a few weeks and had gone to the hospital, trusting my assistant to "keep the home fires burning." I had not known whether I would be able to keep afloat financially and had told some of my customers I might have to close up shop if I didn't recover quickly. Fortunately, I got well soon and didn't lose my shop, but later I found out that six women, including Mrs. Auchincloss, had gotten together and decided that each of them would contribute $200 to help me out till I was on my feet again. I was glad I didn't have to accept the money, but I was as touched as if I had.

One thing I respected Mrs. Auchincloss for was the way she had cooperated in keeping her daughters in a close relationship with their father. She was a very unselfish woman, and was always guided by what was best for the children, rather than what she might have preferred.

Remembering my own children's reactions to the visits of their father, from whom I was divorced, I felt especially close to Mrs. Auchincloss because I had heard many stories of Jacqueline's deep attachment to her father.

When they lived in New York, he would come to visit his daughters and take them out for a day in the country with dogs, dolls and ice cream cones. As a mother myself, who waited at home and afterwards listened to the children's excited reports of a day's outing with Daddy, I knew how it must have been for Jackie and her mother and her sister.

But getting back to those nostalgic days of the early fifties, that mirror saw a lot. I used to tell Mrs. Auchincloss there was only one thing wrong with her mirror—it showed every wrinkle in a face or a dress.

It saw some funny sights, too. It saw a long-suffering chauffeur having to make two or three trips every time one of my customers, "Mrs. Clothes Horse," came for a fitting. He would stagger in, hardly able to see around the heap of dresses, and then go back for another load. That woman, still a part of Washington social life, had so many clothes she could have dressed a chorus line of twenty-four girls with five changes during the show. It would take three or four hours of steady fitting after one of her shopping sprees. My other customers would get tired of waiting past their appointed time.

Once she was highly insulted when I turned to take care of another customer who had come for a scheduled appointment to fit a single dress.

As I fitted the other woman's dress, Mrs. Clothes Horse berated me, saying she didn't want me to permit any other customers to come in while she was there. "I can pay you more than anybody," she snapped. "I can give you more business than anyone else. If you have *me* you don't need anyone else."

I felt sorry to have my other customer hear such rude boasting. But she, an older, distinguished, professional woman, was kind enough to pretend she had heard nothing and continued to leaf through a magazine.

Mrs. Clothes Horse and I soon parted company. *She* could afford me all right but, emotionally, I couldn't afford *her*. The mirror saw it all and seemed to approve when I showed Mrs. Clothes Horse the door.

The mirror also witnessed another customer, a prominent socialite, dashing out of the shop one day in her slip. One of my helpers saw her, thought she had lost her mind and rushed out after her with a coat. I rushed out too— we were like three blind mice. But it wasn't the "farmer's wife" who was chasing us—it was the police.

"Stop!" she shouted. "Don't you dare take my car." She had parked illegally and the policemen were about to tow her car away. So, with the coat over her shoulders, Mrs. Anonymous sought a new parking spot. The cops, who got an eyeful of a fine figure partially covered by frilly lace, couldn't keep their faces straight long enough to give her a ticket or bawl her out.

My dear mirror was shocked—really shocked—by Mrs. Nameless. She came to her fittings without proper undergarments. Actually, without any undergarments. She knew how to comport herself at the White House and was a frequent visitor there, but she didn't know the slightest thing about decorum elsewhere.

One day when she came for a fitting, she opened her purse triumphantly, took out a pair of black panties and said, "I brought these as a concession to you." I had told her at the time of her previous fitting, "I'm afraid I will stick a pin into you. I do wish you would wear some undergarments for your fittings. Otherwise I'm afraid I can't fit you."

She had protested, "They will make wrinkles in my dress if I do." I had to admit her clothes fitted with nary a wrinkle as though they had been painted on.

She was really a beautiful woman with a perfectly stunning figure and, with the panties on this time, I enjoyed fitting her. When we were finished, she calmly took off the panties again, started toward the door, turned and, waving them gaily, called, "Happy days." As she reached the door, she stuffed them back into her purse and said briskly, "Now I'm off to the White House."

I know you will find this story hard to believe, but it is absolutely true that when she dashed off to the White House her only undergarments were two garters! And my mirror can so testify.

Speaking of decorum in ladies—or the lack of it—makes me remember that Jackie once questioned some men about manners. She asked, "What do you think is the sign of a gentleman?" to which one man answered quite honestly, "I'm not qualified to speak. Heavens, I'm no gentleman!"

That might have been the case, too, with a nice-looking man who came in and said he'd like to order six dresses— two daytime, two cocktail and two evening. I was thrilled. That was indeed a big order.

I noticed he kept preening himself in the mirror and I was anxious to get him out of there before my next female customer arrived. "When would your wife like to come in and be fitted?" I asked.

"They're not for my wife," he said, sounding annoyed at the question. "They're for me." My mirror almost fell off the wall. "I'm a female impersonator and I need some dresses," he explained.

Even so, I felt it best to tell him that I was leaving for a vacation and, since only my assistant would be around to finish the assignment, I couldn't take new business. I could just see the expressions on the faces of my regular customers if a man in an evening gown suddenly popped out from behind my screen.

The confidence my customers had in me was quite often amazing. I'll never forget the time TV commentator Jerry

Strong called me about two days before a very fashionable ball and asked me to make a dress for his wife to wear. There were to be no fittings, because he wanted to surprise her. I asked him what color it should be and he answered, "The whole thing is entirely up to you, so have fun!"

After talking to him I realized that I had only partial measurements for Jimma as I had not yet made an evening gown for her. I had her muslin form, of course, but even so, an evening gown should have at least *one* fitting for length. I solved that problem *à la française* by making the dress shorter in front, with a little train in the back. It was blue satin with silver beading on the bodice and skirt.

I think I would be safe in saying that it was one of Jimma's favorite dresses. Amazingly enough, it fit her perfectly, even though she didn't see it until the very afternoon of the day she was to wear it to the ball.

Also among her favorites was a "four-way" outfit that I designed for her to take on a trip to Europe. This consisted of a sheath dress, with an over-blouse and reversible cape, that was practically a wardrobe in itself. Something like this is almost indispensable for women who travel.

As I fitted other *Times-Herald* reporters in front of my mirror, I learned that Jackie, although not particularly interested in politics, was especially intrigued with everything about the White House. She was always asking the White House reporters, male and female, about their jobs and telling them they were lucky to go there. Everything about the White House was exciting to her. "How was it there?" she'd ask them about their White House visits covering a press conference or a social event. "Did you get to see Mrs. Truman?"

She asked the reporters and photographers if they got to see other parts of the White House. "Do they let you in the family's rooms or just in the President's office? Can you wander from the Press Room now and then or do the guards stop you?"

Once, in May, she stationed herself outside the White House and asked the tourists, as they came out, what they had liked best. She wrote up their glowing accounts of how beautiful the interior was—the Blue Room, the Green Room, the Red Room and the magnificent East Room with its chandeliers and the ornamented grand piano.

One visitor, however, was most impressed by the White House servants—"They looked so spick-and-span."

My mirror, unfortunately, was not a crystal ball and could not show us that those spick-and-span servants would some day be Jackie's.

And right after that question, she went around asking women, "Which First Lady would you liked to have been?"

One woman's answer simply staggered me. Without hesitation she had replied, "Lincoln's. I could have prevented the assassination. He was tired that night, and I wouldn't have let him go to the theater. I always thought if I'd been his wife I'd have prevented his death."

I'm sure the mirror disapproved of a particular mother who would come in with her daughter and dictate what she would wear. The daughter was around Jackie's age— twenty-two or twenty-three—and her mother made life miserable for her. She would never let the girl come to the shop alone, afraid that either she or I might express an unorthodox idea. This girl was athletic, loved horseback riding and outdoor life and didn't care at all about getting dressed up.

Her mother was very feminine and liked to go to parties and dressed her daughter in the same buttons and bows she liked for herself. Instead of boosting the girl's confidence in herself the mother was actually giving the girl an inferiority complex. I watched that poor girl balloon up twenty or thirty pounds—probably from eating too many sweets to compensate for her frustration. But what could the mirror or I do?

Mrs. Auchincloss certainly wasn't that kind of mother. She let Jackie grow up by herself and never tried to keep her under her thumb.

The mirror was especially kind to Mrs. Auchincloss, who dressed according to her own taste and let her daughters dress according to theirs. Mrs. Auchincloss looked extremely well in her softly feminine clothes and the mirror beamed back at her with a special sparkle when she wore cheerful and colorful prints.

She had let her daughters choose for themselves ever since they graduated from look-alike sister outfits. She had dressed them in identical clothes to show them she loved them equally. Jackie had learned by trial and error to choose things she would like not just for a day. She had even been trusted to pick her own party dresses and once, with an unlimited budget for a gown, had picked a modestly priced dress from a rack, to the amazement and pride of her mother.

Jackie knew a price tag does not necessarily reflect good taste, and that good taste has no price tag.

Once the mirror watched Jackie and me design a whole evening gown around some lovely lace that had come from France. The mirror reflected approval as Jackie stood tall before it, with the lace flowers, which we had cut from the strip, pinned on one by one to make a long lazy-flowing, willowy pattern down from one side of the strapless bodice to the hem of the other side of the skirt.

To soothe the nerves of my customers while they were undergoing an important fitting I kept soft music playing on my radio, which was hidden from sight. The tranquility would be broken, however, first by the telephone and then by the buzzer, which meant that Margy had not been able

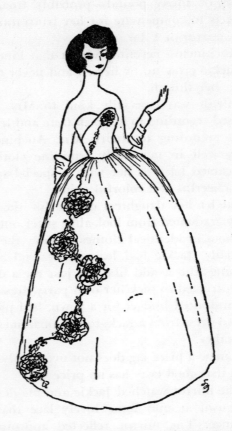

Often we'd leaf through French fashion
magazines looking for interesting treatments.
This dress was designed around the theme of
lace flowers which Jackie had brought from
Paris. I cut them from the strip. My mirror
watched us pin them on, one by one.

to satisfy the customer and she still wanted to talk to me. "How in the world do you keep your train of thought?" Jackie would ask. "That buzzer is as distracting as a flash bulb."

Jacqueline was very sensitive to music and would comment on liking my choices whenever something with a Parisian touch was on, something like *April in Paris* or one of Offenbach's gay pieces. She also liked classical and semi-classical music, and I could tell she knew much more about the subject than I did.

She tried to think of ways in which the interest of Americans in opera could be stimulated and asked the members of the Metropolitan Opera Company's *Madame Butterfly* cast, "Do you think foreign language opera should be sung in English in this country?"

Every once in a while she would seek out members of the Washington National Symphony to ask some question about music, and in line with her interest in ballet she went not once, but several times, to interview the members of the Ballet Russe while they were rehearsing. And she would interview other dance troupes, like that of José Greco.

She asked them what they thought of American dances such as the Charleston and the jitterbug, but the question that most amused me, and showed Jackie's curiosity about them, was when she asked what they thought about *while* they were dancing.

I had a feeling she hoped for great uplifting thoughts, more in keeping with the depth and sweep of the music, but they gave such disappointing answers as, "The noise," or, "I don't think of anything."

I told Jackie what *I* had thought about the day I had first performed a toe dance in front of my father. I had thought about how scared I was because my father disapproved of dancing. It was a May dance at the school and since this was a Methodist school my father had felt perfectly safe in letting Mother make me a costume for the May Day Festival.

He was sitting in the front row, very proudly, as I started my dance, and little did he suspect that suddenly in the middle of the dance I would fling away my long, flowing skirt and dance in the briefest of tights. I can still see the look of horror on his face as I twirled by, trying not to see him, yet looking anyway.

Jackie knew all about the look of horror on an adult's face because once at school she had accidentally-on-purpose dropped a pie in the lap of a teacher, and she had seen a look of horror that must have been very much like my father's.

"I must remember that and some day do a column for you on the wickedness of dancing," she said, laughing.

I used to think Jackie must get a little kick out of startling some of the people she questioned, just as she had liked to startle her teachers. She asked, for example, "If you were to be electrocuted tomorrow morning, what would you order for your last meal?" I said, off the record, that I didn't believe I'd be interested in ordering.

And I was surprised, to say the least, when she asked attractive young girls if they would rather be "an old man's darling or a young man's slave?" Only one girl said, brazenly, that she would choose the old man's money, hoping to outlive him. Most of the girls showed a more healthy attitude, being willing to marry the younger man in hopes of changing him for the better before he made a slave of her.

Another shocker, which she sprang on married people, was, "If you had legally been declared dead, for one reason or another, and returned to find your spouse married to your best friend, what would you do?"

Then, on the other hand, Jackie's questions could be as

sweet and guileless as the one she asked her little half-brother, James Auchincloss, at his birthday party that spring: "What do you like most about birthday parties?" But innocent questions, too, could sometimes lead to shocking answers.

Little Jamie, who was tougher on his fifth birthday than he would probably ever be again, said with utter frankness that he liked his own parties best, that he was glad he was five because now he was "big enough to shoot my bow and arrow in the little boys' eyes" and that on his next birthday he wanted to be "14½ years old" so he could be older than all his sisters.

My mirror got a good look at Jamie one day when Jackie brought him and little Janet—perhaps six-and-a-half years old then—along to her fitting and I got a new insight into Jackie's character.

"I hope you don't mind," Jackie said with a proprietory grin, "but, as you see, I'm baby-sitting today." I could see she was prepared because she had some children's books instead of her usual armload of books in English and French fashion magazines.

The mirror looked the pair over and found them very healthy, very competitive youngsters, each not about to let the other get ahead. And I looked at Jackie and saw a new side of her—a young woman aglow with maternal tenderness. She read to them quietly until another customer had left. Then she saw that they were both settled with their own books. This girl would enjoy motherhood, I thought, surprised. She'd probably make a great mother —and a glamorous one.

While she was being fitted, Jackie kept one eye on the little ones, watching for signs of mutiny. Every time there was an indication that book-snatching or fist-fighting was in the offing, due to Janet's lording it over Jamie because of her superiority in understanding the pictures and printing, a word from Jackie was all it took to quiet them.

"I was just as bad as Janet when I was small," she said. "I really was hard on Lee and riding herd all the time." So anxious had she been to correct her little sister, Caroline Lee, that once when Lee had said something nice about how a workman looked, Jackie had corrected her right in front of him, saying it wasn't true and that the man looked just like a fox or a weasel. Jackie confessed she had always regretted this unkind remark. But the main thing was that Jackie could still remember what it was like to be a child, and felt a tenderness toward all the young and helpless—human and animal.

As Jackie got dressed behind the screen, I had a chance to get acquainted with the children and I told Janet and Jamie I had enjoyed reading about them in the papers. Jamie acted surprised that anyone so far from home knew about him. "I am keeping your birthday story as a souvenir," I said.

As they left, Jamie ran back to say goodbye to me. And after he was gone I saw the mirror had a souvenir, too— one happy little hand print. I hated to wash it off.

And I felt the mirror wanted it left on, too.

CHAPTER 8

A TOUCH OF POLITICS

I WAS PROUD when a wardrobe of my clothes went to the Democratic Convention. Aha, I thought, as the ticket shaped up to "Stevenson and Sparkman," I may soon be dressing the Number Two woman of the whole country. I was thinking of Mrs. Sparkman's position if her husband, Senator John Sparkman, won the election for the Vice-Presidency. Stevenson had no wife. Wouldn't that make my customer, Mrs. Sparkman, even more important in Washington? Of course, everyone expected that Adlai Stevenson's sister, Mrs. Ives, would be his official hostess and that she would come to live in the White House, but it was safe to assume that Mrs. Sparkman would have a greater social burden than if there were a First Lady "through marriage."

Jackie had again dismissed the second political convention with a mild-as-milk question, "What do you think of the nomination of Governor Stevenson?" But in spite of the fact that she wasn't going out looking for political arguments, some of the people she interviewed brought politics home to her.

One man, when asked what was most important to him in all the world, said bluntly, "I am living to see Senator Taft elected President."

"If Stevenson gets it and I become known as the 'dressmaker who sews for Mrs. John Sparkman,' watch my business grow," I told the girls.

But they were about as disinterested in politics and political figures as Jackie seemed to be. They were spectacularly unimpressed when I told them that the person they had just seen leaving my fitting room was the famous Mrs. Such-and-Such.

Once Jimi almost bumped into Mrs. Dean Acheson and made only a cursory apology. "You should be polite to everyone," I scolded. "And you were hardly even civil to the wife of one of the most prominent men in the country."

The girls were used to famous people because they baby-sat for them. I couldn't get over how calm Sylvia had been when she got a chance to see President Truman in person. People had been lining the hot streets and waiting wearily for a glimpse of the President as he drove by with a foreign dignitary on the way from the airport. Sylvia, as luck would have it, was baby-sitting at the home where the President came later to relax and hold conversations with the notable foreign guest, in the beautiful garden with its cool swimming pool. Sylvia had taken the family's toddlers to the pool and so had seen Mr. Truman close up.

"What did you think of the President?" I asked.

"Oh, he looked like a very nice man," she said, casually. Nothing more. Period.

But when Jackie was in the fitting room Sylvia was like

a jack-in-the-box, popping in to answer the telephone, popping in to ask if I had called her. Any excuse, I realized, to get another look at Jackie. But then, Jackie wasn't a mere President. *She* was the inquiring camera girl. You couldn't beat that.

My two teen-agers made the most of every opportunity and once they were so tickled because they stumped Jacqueline on a riddle: "Why does worry kill more people than work does?"

She couldn't think of the right answer. "Because more people worry than work," they told her gleefully, and waited to see if Jackie would quote this in her column. But they were doomed to disappointment because Jackie never asked riddles in her interviews—teasing and provocative questions, yes, but not riddles.

I had worked for two months helping Mrs. Sparkman and her daughter, Julia—Mrs. Tazewell Taylor Shepard, Jr.—get their complete wardrobes ready for the Democratic Convention and had made the many new things they needed for the hectic days and nights.

Mrs. Sparkman required versatile two-piece ensembles so she could go from the daytime Convention sessions directly to politico-social late afternoon and dinner engagements. Her color choices were light blue, beige and pale green. In contrast to her petite daintiness, her daughter was tall, slender and chose more dramatic styles.

Today Julia's husband, Captain Shepard, is at the White House every day as Naval Aide to the husband of the girl who came in and out of my shop and avoided politics— Jacqueline Kennedy.

What I recall most about Mrs. Sparkman—a lovely person to work with—was the fact that she was so afraid of dogs. Before she would even enter my shop, she'd peep in the front door and say, "Please . . ." and I would know to put Taffy away.

I told my girls that if the Stevenson-Sparkman ticket won the election, I would bet that Jackie did a column asking people, "What advice would you give the wife of the Vice-President in overcoming her fear of dogs?"

I was getting to be like Jackie, seeing a question in every human foible.

Jackie, incidentally, had switched to lighter colored accessories for summer: a light brown—almost beige— shoulder bag and comfortable but good looking matching pumps. A collarless, beige dress, with a little tab in front, like a tie, gave Jackie that tailored look she wanted.

I noticed that even in summer she preferred materials that held their shape, instead of wearing the voiles or other flimsy materials that soon became limp and made their wearers look even hotter. She wore no eyeletted materials for work and shunned jewelry, which can give an uncomfortable, cluttered look in hot weather.

Jackie proved she was no slave to fashion even when it came to shoes. She never wore white shoes in summer, knowing they make a woman's foot look larger.

I heard that part of the time, while keeping cool, Jackie was sitting down at the *Times-Herald* building, sketching the reporters and photographers as *they* tried to keep cool. She sketched them as she saw them—their feet on the desk, reading the paper, lounging at the water fountain, napping across a couple of chairs.

I also heard that one of her special friends on the paper was a collateral descendant of Edgar Allan Poe. Her name was Vylla Poe Wilson and Jackie would perch on her desk in the City Room and hear about the old days there. Mrs. Wilson could recall the years when the paper had been owned by William Randolph Hearst, who seldom used his office in the Hearst Bureau and she, a fledgling reporter, had taken to using it for him. All went well until she made one mistake—she forgetfully left some love letters from her beau in Mr. Hearst's desk. When he found them she lost a good office and had to go back to being an ordinary cub reporter.

Mrs. Wilson could top Jackie's experience in becoming an inquiring photographer, without a moment's previous experience, with one of her own job experiences. One day Vylla's editor had called her in and announced with no preamble, "You are now the art editor." She thought a moment and then said, "Well, I'm glad I'm not the sports editor." So she'd gone out to learn a new field from scratch, just as Jackie had done.

As a respite from my excitement over the nominations, I turned more than ever to Jackie's column. It was the best "escape" literature in Washington, and I searched the *Times-Herald* avidly for her delightful Q's and A's.

She asked, "What do you think flying saucers really are?"

And "What do you like or dislike about your boss?"

I had to tease her about one column, though. In it she'd asked people what country they would like to live in if they didn't live in the United States. I had hunted rapidly through the six interviews to see how many wanted to live in France. I could imagine her searching diligently for people who shared her appreciation for that country.

Alas, not one soul chose France. One wanted to go to Sweden, one to Belgium, one to England—"because it's most like America"—one to Australia, one to Newfoundland and one woman even wanted to go to Norway because they keep cool with sod roofs and are smart enough to tether their goats up there.

On August 12 there was one I loved! "Would you like to crash high society?" I could tell that none of the persons she interviewed that day had any inkling that the demurely dressed girl in a simple shepherd plaid shirtwaist dress, slung with camera and shoulder bag, was high society herself, even though, to the fashion-conscious eye her simple pumps would look suspiciously custom made.

She asked this question in a run-down section of G Street. One man said he would like to mingle with the upper crust because all his friends told him he looked like a socialite. He said he'd like to throw a party and invite the President and Lana Turner and "Margaret Truman would come out in a slinky dress and sing." Then he added a wonderful human interest touch. He said he'd invite all his G Street friends but he'd make them go to Emily Post first to find out how to behave. Of course, he didn't feel *he* needed any pointers.

A counterman said he'd already been a part of the swanky set because once he had $36,000. But he had thrown it all away having a good time—and he'd do it again. His idea of being rich was to ride around in a taxi all day—in the back seat.

A few men she interviewed wanted nothing to do with high society—one because he didn't like going around in those "monkey suits," one because he couldn't stomach those garden parties and another because he didn't like the people one met in high society. "Some of them," he said, "are worse than the people down here. I'll stick to high society G Street style. I wouldn't like associating with Tommy Manville. He'd be a bad influence even on G Street."

Still another man said he had more fun "just talking to the guys on the corner" than he would have at a diplomatic function but added, magnanimously, "if they're happy that way, I don't see why they shouldn't live that way."

That, I told Jackie, laughing, was true democracy.

Another kind of democracy was going on in Massachusetts and Jackie was there in spirit. That was where the Kennedy family, or at least a good part of it, were helping their "favorite son," politically speaking, to campaign for the Senate. I must say that when I found out that Jack Kennedy was one of nine children, my sympathy, as a fellow one-of-nine, was all with him.

But the Kennedy family had not been as lucky as my Sells family, which had *not* been saddened by the death of any of its members. In the Kennedy family there had been two great tragedies, both involving airplanes. The eldest son, Joseph, who was a Navy pilot, had been shot down over the English Channel during World War II and a daughter, Kathleen, who had married the Marquess of Hartington and lived in England, had lost her life in a plane crash a few years after the war.

I think it was these tragedies which knit the Kennedy family more closely together and made them work as a team with and for each other, realizing, perhaps, more than others how precious each one was to the entire family.

Eunice and Jean both lived in Chicago where their father owned the Merchandise Mart. They both came to Massachusetts to help their brother. Patricia, who was working in TV production in New York, left her career to aid Jack, and even Mother Kennedy, who was vacationing abroad, came back to help.

As I heard it, the mother was the best campaigner of them all because she had grown up in politics as the daughter of the Mayor of Boston and was used to talking to anyone and everyone about any subject close to their hearts. Besides, she was practically the star attraction because all the women wanted to meet and talk with the wife of the former Ambassador to the Court of St. James.

So women came from far and wide to attend the new kind of political rallies: "Boston tea parties" with the Boston Kennedys, at which Mrs. Kennedy would say a few words and the three sisters would say a few words and the candidate—if he was there—would say a few words and everyone would enjoy tea and tiny sandwiches.

The leader of this family troupe was Robert Kennedy, who was just out of law school, and once when every member of his valiant gang was speaking elsewhere *he* had to make a speech. He got up and said something like this: "My brother couldn't get here in time to address you. My mother couldn't get here. My sister Eunice couldn't get here. My sister Jean couldn't make it. My sister Pat couldn't make it. And, as I said, the candidate couldn't get here. But if he *were* here, my brother Jack would tell you that Lodge has a very poor voting record. I thank you." That was the end of the speeches for that night and the crowd loved it and settled for shooting questions at the very intelligent lawyer.

Jackie, I could see, was intrigued by this close-knit family and wondering from afar, as I was, what it was like to attend such an affair. Of course the fact that Jack Kennedy was a handsome bachelor helped bring in the curious mother-daughter teams, but if that worried Jackie, she didn't show it.

It was not until August was well along that Jackie got enough into the spirit of Kennedy's campaign to ask an out-and-out political question concerning vote-getting.

She asked, "Do a candidate's looks influence your vote?" The answers were a great lesson in practical politics and I was sure that a certain Senatorial candidate was as interested as were the ladies in my fitting room.

The men said the looks of a candidate did not matter to them but added that they were aware that, naturally, women were impressionable. And women frankly admitted that a candidate's looks *did* matter. One woman, a career girl, put it so well that it seemed to apply especially to one JFK. She said, "I don't go for the guy with the big toothy

Elk Lodge No. 35 grin. He has to look helpless, as if he really needs my vote."

Well, there was certainly something appealingly helpless looking about this particular candidate. Articles were being written about Kennedy's special charm, which made every woman want to "either marry him or mother him." He looked as though he needed not only votes but meals, and a mop of hair falling over his forehead certainly added to his untended, boyish look.

I smiled as I thought how the people Jackie was questioning probably thought she was referring to the Presidential race—Eisenhower and Nixon versus Stevenson and Sparkman—rather than to any State one, but I was sure her thoughts were very much on Massachusetts.

I started to feel that the Congressman was finally getting through to Jacqueline on politics because as the compaign of 1952 became more intense she was starting to ask questions such as: "Should a candidate's wife campaign with her husband?"

I wondered whether there was a personal meaning in that question and I was also starting to wonder whether some of the questions were inspired by Mr. Kennedy or were questions whose answers he was especially interested in. On October 22, for example, she asked, "Is Truman's whistle stop tour helping Stevenson?"

Another question I felt Kennedy might have been interested in was whether people thought that televising the political conventions would lead to more intelligent and enlightened voting.

In September, *Life* magazine had a big spread on a Kennedy tea and garden party. The story said he had greeted 20,000 women voters and ballyhooed: "Young Kennedy seeks to win women, appeals with new and potent weapon, political teas to win women's votes."

In one of their photographs, a woman was shown sitting all alone, with a mourning veil over her face. She was a supporter of Lodge. This woman certainly had extra-sensory perception, mourning the defeat of Lodge in advance.

Election time was upon the nation in that November of 1952, and I didn't see how Jacqueline's friend could wrest the Senate seat from Henry Cabot Lodge. Everyone was predicting a Republican landslide and in my shop I hardly heard a person who didn't say, "I like Ike," or, "Ike's chances look good."

Even those who said, "Stevenson is the better man," added rather mournfully, "but I wish he had a wife and were a little more colorful."

In the eleventh hour, Jacqueline was busy asking campaign questions like mad. She wanted to know how people thought the election was going. She asked older newspapermen what their most dramatic election memories were and, lo and behold! the number one person in her column on that subject was Arthur Krock of the *New York Times* —who had helped her get her job.

He recalled the Wilson-Hughes campaign of 1916. "I was managing editor of the *Louisville Courier-Journal and Times*," Krock told Jackie. "Wilson conceded at 11 P.M. I kept an eye on Ohio and at 6 A.M. I dressed the front page with a row of roosters—Democratic victory symbols. When the California and Minnesota returns were in, Charles Evans Hughes, the man who went to bed thinking he was President, awakened to find he wasn't."

Jackie even sought out Washington's top society hostess to ask this question: "With which Presidential candidate would you rather be marooned on a desert island?" Mrs. Morris Cafritz gave a most hilarious answer. "I'm a very social person, you know. I think being stranded with either one would get a bit tiresome after a while. What I'd really love is to be marooned with both of them, on the same island at the same time. They mightn't like it so much, but I think it would be divine."

I remember that Jackie went to the Embassy Room of the Statler Hotel and asked the waiters if they had any interesting recollections of past Presidents they had served there. One said that FDR had always called him "Charlie" every time he saw him although Charlie wasn't his name. But he'd been afraid to correct the President. Another remembered that Truman didn't care much for wine.

Election night found Jackie at the Republican election headquarters asking the happy people celebrating Eisenhower's victory, "How do you feel now?"

And with typical Jackie luck she'd managed to run into —of all people—a cousin of Stevenson, who was chortling over his cousin's defeat. He had let her take his picture and in great high spirits had given her a quote:

"Oh, I'm overjoyed! I'm inexpressibly happy! I've been in a dither for twenty years, hoping and praying and working in the Republican party. And now I feel this is the answer to my prayers. You know Adlai Stevenson's my cousin. He's a very fine gentleman but still I am not feeling sorry for any of my relatives tonight."

It must have pained Jackie to take down his words because she already knew what it meant to plug for a Democratic candidate against the Republican tide in her family.

And eight years later when her sister, Nina Auchincloss Steers, severed family bonds by backing Richard Nixon, while the rest of her family supported her husband, John Kennedy, she must have remembered that night at Republican headquarters.

Yes, '52 held some good lessons for Jackie, though in the big picture it was just a touch of politics.

CHAPTER 9

CHRISTMAS, 1952

WHAT A RIOTOUS time there was in Washington after Eisenhower's landslide returns came in! Jackie was in the thick of it as a girl reporter.

The day after election a Washington doctor who had backed Eisenhower got a free ride in a wheelbarrow around the White House. Pushing the wheelbarrow was a nurse who wore a sign admitting she had lost an election bet by supporting Adlai. The gaily festooned wheelbarrow also had a sign: "I've waited twenty years for this ride."

Jackie's paper featured a picture from Boston showing a big sign over a door. The woman who lived there had printed just two words, "Thank God."

But Jackie was, I am sure, more interested in reading about how one lone Democratic bachelor Congressman had bucked the strong Republican tide to win a smashing victory over Henry Cabot Lodge, Jr. Kennedy had gotten 1,207,000 votes—a margin of 68,753 over Lodge.

Everyone said it had been a miracle and it showed what family teamwork could do.

Well, I thought, Jackie and her mother can both be happy about this election. They both got their favorite candidate.

But election or no election, the daily papers were published and Jackie kept working hard. Some of her questions continued to have a political angle: "Who would you like to see in President Eisenhower's Cabinet?" and, "Do you think Eisenhower should confer with General MacArthur before going to Korea?"

She even showed a new interest in the international situation by asking, "What four Americans would you name or delegate to the UN to match Russia's team of Vishinsky, Gromyko, Zorin and Zorubin?"

But the questions and answers I, as a dressmaker, read with greatest interest were those concerned with the effect Mamie Eisenhower's personality would have on the national scene. I have to smile, knowing how Jacqueline so dislikes publicity about her fashions and tastes now that she is in the White House, when I remember she was guilty of focusing the same type of attention on her predecessor. In fact, one of the first things she wanted to know from the average woman after the 1952 election was, "Do you think Mamie Eisenhower's bangs will become a nationwide fashion?"

The answers she received from housewives should certainly have prepared her for her own goldfish bowl ordeal. One woman said she'd already cut bangs on her daughter, "so she will be in style."

Another said she was sure that bangs would now be all the rage, explaining, "People mimic everything, even if it's not becoming. They want to follow the leader like a lot of sheep." A third woman said, "I've got bangs already, but they're under my hat so you can't see them." And a fourth confessed she had tried to wear them but they looked terrible on her. She added, "I better not say anything against them though. Mrs. Ike might call me up and raise Hail Columbia."

And as our First Lady now bemoans the fact that photographers take pictures of her children with telephoto lenses and that the interest of reporters makes it impossible to give them privacy, I am sure she remembers when she was a part of the newspaper gang looking for a fresh approach to our important national figures from the viewpoint of their children.

The votes were hardly counted before she'd scooped the other papers by seeking out Patricia Nixon, six-year-old daughter of the new Vice-President, in front of her home at 4801 Tilden Street. "What do you think of Senator Nixon now?" she had asked.

Little Tricia, as she was called, had promptly given one of the best quotes I ever read: "He's always away. If he's famous why can't he stay home? See this picture? That's a coming home present I made for Daddy. Julie did one too, but she can't color as well as me. All my class was voting for Eisenhower, but I told them I was just going to vote for Daddy."

The interview made a hit with her editor and her readers, who definitely included me, as well as practically every last customer.

She followed up with another child's-eye-view story that was so good her editor put it on the front page. It was a wonderful story about the complications of being the nieces of a President.

To get it, Jackie had waited outside the John Eaton public school for two little girls, at 35th and Lowell Streets, N.W., and had walked them home. As they walked, Jackie had sketched them and the wonderful squiggle drawing, showing ten-year-old Mamie Moore and eleven-year-old Ellen Moore carrying their school books, had appeared with the story.

Young Mamie was complaining that reporters called the house asking for "Mamie" and her mother, instead of calling her to the phone, told them Mamie wasn't there. "My mother thought they meant my Aunt Mamie," she said, "but how did she know they didn't mean me?" Mamie had a further complaint that "only three people in my class knew Uncle Ike was my uncle." But she added that since she had brown hair and bangs "everybody said I look like Aunt Mamie and so now they all know."

But poor Ellen, who was not named after anybody famous and didn't even have bangs, was really sad. She pointed to her hair to show the absence of bangs. "Nobody knows who I am," she said.

On the brighter side, Mamie reported that a girl in class had suggested she tell the teacher that unless she gave her good grades the President of the United States, her uncle, would "throw her off the school board." But, after all, Mamie reflected aloud, she didn't think it would do any good "because if Uncle Ike heard that, he'd just tell my mother and would she get mad!"

I was as proud of that front page story as if I were still back on the *Port Gibson Reveille* in Mississippi and had written it myself. When I heard that the girls' mother, Mrs. Gordon Moore, Jr., had called the editor to complain about the interview which had been obtained without her permission, I was on Jackie's side. The unwritten law of the newspaper world is, "The public has a right to know." After all, it had been a delightful story that showed Mrs. Moore was a good mother and what harm had been done?

Jackie was feeling badly about it, however, and told several people how sorry she was, adding, "It must be just terrible to be so prominent that your children are exposed to so much publicity." It was typical of Jackie not to want to hurt anyone and to be able to see both sides of an issue.

A hard-boiled reporter would have enjoyed her triumph without regrets. Actually, Jackie had done only what she had done many times before, seeking out children and getting quotes from them. "Children make the best stories," she always told me. Hadn't she gone out to the schools and interviewed children on the day that summer vacation had begun, and again on the day that vacation was over? That had been in Hyattsville, Maryland. And hadn't she gone to a primary school in McLean, Virginia, to find out "What makes little boys so bad?" And hadn't she come back with the gem of a comment from a six-year-old boy: "They're not bad. It's little girls that hit you hardest. They're badder."

She certainly had. Jackie was no stranger to the schools of the whole area of the District of Columbia. She had even gone to the Mitchell Park playground as Father's Day approached to see what children were going to do "to make your father happy on Father's Day."

Jackie was fast becoming the *Times-Herald's* expert on child opinion rating—the Gallup of the five-to-eleven set.

She was also becoming somewhat psychic about timing.

Once in December I kidded Jacqueline about causing men to beat their wives when her column tied in nicely with a story across the page. In answering Jackie's question, "What is your worst fault as a husband?" one man, with tongue in cheek, said, "I'm too good to my wife. That's my worst fault. Women like to be mistreated. Probably all the wives of husbands that beat them are happier than my Katherine."

The story across the page from Jackie's column was entitled "Wife Beaters Can Be Sued for Damages," and told how a woman, who had three ribs fractured by her husband, a man who evidently thought as "Katherine's" husband did, was demanding $50,000 in damages. An act of 1874, which was upheld by an Illinois court, was the precedent on which her plea was based.

Yes, Jacqueline certainly had a knack for timing!

The Congressman was now a Senator-elect, and in the holiday season of 1952 Jacqueline really had a holiday glow. She was asking little children what they wanted for Christmas, and I began to have an inkling that what *she* wanted was the Senator. She was more clothes-conscious and was again designing more gowns.

She came tearing in, saying, "I have this t-rrific idea for a dress." She gave me an idea in a rough sketch of the effect she wanted to achieve. It did even more for the bust line than my magic darts did. She had beaten me at my own game.

Together we worked out the design for a white ball gown to be worn with a red stole—a wonderful Christmas touch.

Jackie had brought in eight yards of beautiful white satin and two-and-a-half yards of red velvet and now it was up to me to figure out how to cut the dress and the red velvet stole. It was Jackie's idea to have a long, floor-to-floor stole, with much fullness at the bottom. This I managed by a wonderful trick, which everyone of you can try for yourselves.

I took the two-and-a-half yards of the red velvet which was 45 inches wide, and cut it diagonally. Then I slid the two pieces apart. Holding one piece to the floor—allowing material to turn under, of course—I drew the material up to the back of the neck. Then I put the other piece on the other side, also reaching the floor, with allowance for turning under, and pinned the two pieces together at the back of the neck, so I would know where to sew them. The stole was backed with the same shade of red silk.

To the best of my knowledge, Jacqueline was the first person to wear this type of floor-to-floor stole in Washington, and it was entirely her own idea. I only had the headache of trying to figure out how to make it.

This stole was such an innovation that, with her permission, I displayed it on a form in my shop. It created a sensation among my customers. Soon they were wanting similar stoles for themselves.

For the dress, I first cut a new muslin form for the top because that was the part that had the tricky fitting. I started just as one would start to make a plain strapless bodice. Then, to form this type of bodice, which is particularly flattering to the figure, I cut two bias folds of material, one for each side. In the muslin I put small pleats in each piece at the bottom, facing away from the center.

In the finished garment these two petal-like pieces were cut of double material.

To explain in further detail, in this dress the satin was pinned close to the body to make a smooth foundation. Then over the bust line a second bodice was shaped to stand away from the figure, forming the petal effect.

For the foundation of this dress, I used two layers of heavy material, similar to muslin, which I cross-stitched back and forth to give it more body. It was cut to fit the figure exactly, so that it served as a bra inside the dress. Then the satin bodice was attached to this foundation at the side seams only.

There was a seamline at the waist and the skirt was cut in six large panels, or gores, which were fitted at the waist to lie smoothly and enlarged at the bottom to fall quite full.

As I usually do, I made the top and the full skirt separately, each piece complete in itself, because this way it is much easier to handle. The waistline measurements of both pieces were checked carefully, as well as all top and bottom seams to see that they matched—all before sewing the bodice and skirt together. The final step was to put the zipper in.

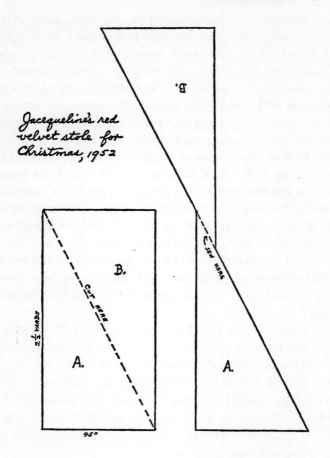

Jacqueline's red
velvet stole for
Christmas, 1952

B.

CUT HERE

SEW HERE

B.

2½ YARDS

A.

A.

45"

Cut a piece of 45" material, about 2½ yds. long, on the
diagonal. Allowing for hems, place 45" width of pieces A &
B on floor and draw up pointed ends to back of neck,
so you will know where to sew them together. Back
with silk in same color as front

The petticoats were attached to the satin skirt at the waistline before the skirt was attached to the bodice. There were three taffeta petticoats, which were also gored, but were gathered just a bit at the waist to give more support. First I had tried a piece of crinoline for a petticoat, but it was too stiff and didn't look right under the satin, so I used the several layers of taffeta instead. Three taffeta petticoats gave it a very nice rustle.

Jackie was very insistent on the complete French construction of this white satin gown. In the French construction the bra and all the petticoats are built right into the dress. Even at that time Jackie had preference for the French type of sewing and the beautiful fit achieved by it.

I remember that the French construction was rather difficult in this dress when I came to handling the second and third layers of petticoats. But after seeing how lovely Jackie looked in it, it was certainly worthwhile—trouble or not.

If I were making the dress today, instead of in 1952, I would not have so much trouble. About four or five years ago a new material, called pellon, came on the market. It is very pliant, but firm. It makes a good backing for wedding gowns, cocktail dresses or evening costumes—any garment which needs body or has a full skirt. As it comes in many different weights, it is a good investment for the do-it-yourself dressmaker.

Nowadays it is almost a full-time job for a dressmaker to keep track of all the new materials which come on the market. There is such a host of them, both in finished fabrics and in foundation ones. And as, today, almost all dresses are partly or completely lined, finding the suitable weight and type of fabric for the lining of each particular dress is quite a job.

In Jacqueline's white satin evening gown the hemline

came just at the instep at the front, to show the tips of the shoes and to give ease in walking. It was slightly longer in back, to skim over the floor.

It was a wonderful season of business for me. Customers kept me sewing happily into the night. Jackie was so pleased with her petal-front gown and stole she didn't even bother to ask me what it was going to cost until she took it home.

I was amused, as she paid me, to think that even though she had received several pay raises and was up to something like $51 a week, her salary would not even pay for half the gown. Jackie can afford her job more than her job can afford her, I thought, and wondered how it would feel to have work as one's hobby.

I was curious to know why Jackie did not wear daytime fur coats, which she could afford, but favored plain black Chesterfields. "One has to be so careful," she said, "because they can make one look so bulky. They're just not for me."

Jackie was in and out of the shop and she sparkled as cheerfully as the tiptop bulb on my Christmas tree. Romance seemed to be having a good effect on her and I could see, reading between the lines, that her column contained certain questions which were meant to have a certain effect on a certain person. For example, one which I considered a "loaded" question appeared about mid-December when Jackie, with no apparent guile, stopped people to ask, "Can you give any reason why a contented bachelor should get married?" I considered asking her how many people she had had to interview before she could come up with six who would say that *every* bachelor should get married.

One woman gave a priceless answer: "Even if a bachelor thinks he's happier running around painting the town, he really isn't. He's just confused." Another girl said if a man didn't marry he was practically a coward who was afraid of women. Another woman used the fear-of-loneliness approach. The gay bachelor wasn't lonely, she said, but "won't he be sorry when he finds himself all alone with nobody to spend his old age with?"

The men were almost as positive. Somewhere Jackie had found a happy fellow who was just about to get married and he vowed he'd never miss his bachelor days. One man aproached marriage from the standpoint of logic and said every man had to do his part to keep the human race going with a couple of kids—he simply wasn't doing his duty to society otherwise.

The only man in the column who started out claiming he was a "contented bachelor" and saw no reason for getting married, ended up, with a bit of prodding from Jackie, by admitting that losing one's freedom must have *some* reward. "I suppose it's compensated for by other things," he said.

The newspapermen and photographers at the *Times-Herald* received Christmas presents that were typically Jackie. She picked those men who needed a lift to their spirits most frequently and gave them packages from the liquor store. Whatever was their favorite brand, they had it. Beautiful ribbons made the unwrapped gift cartons look "t-rrific."

The men drooled as they accepted the boxed bottles but, since Jackie had to go out on assignment, she made them promise to wait till she got back before opening them.

They did.

She did.

Came the great opening.

Milk!! All the bottles were filled with milk.

She had dumped out the whiskey and substituted plain milk. That was Jackie at Christmastide, 1952.

--❧{CHAPTER 10}❧--

A WINTER GAME

NOT UNTIL Christmas and New Year's had come and gone could I catch my breath and see what changes had been wrought in our lives. It seemed that the most important new addition to my fitting room floor was a speck of dog called a Maltese.

We had inherited it by long distance, so to speak, from a customer who had injured her leg and could not take care of the little female puppy which had been brought to her from abroad a few days before her accident. Sylvia had gone to get the dog and, upon returning with it, had rung the bell. When I opened the door and saw what looked like a tiny white muff in Sylvia's hands I gasped, "That's a dog?" I had seen cats that were bigger and with its impressive breed name, "Maltese," I had expected something pretty special.

I admit I gave the bit of fluff a pretty cool welcome, but after I cuddled it in my hands and looked into its beady little eyes, I was hooked. So was Sylvia who, from then on, hardly let me touch the midget creature. And that was how "Chrysanthemum"—the biggest word for a little dog and the hardest for school kids to spell, according to Jackie's column—came to live at our house.

I had thought that Taffy would be jealous, but by the time Jackie came and we were rehashing Christmas we witnessed a minor miracle. Chryssie—we had given up using the spelling bee word but had decided to keep the "y" instead of changing to "i" in spelling her nickname (for, after all, she was a little lady and "Chrissie" might have seemed less feminine)—was tearing back and forth, grabbing poor blind Taffy's ear and then running away, only to return again and tug at her some more. Suddenly Taffy seemed to understand and marched along with Chryssie.

"Good grief," I said. "Chryssie is a seeing eye dog. She's leading Taffy by the ear." And so she was. And as we watched we marveled at how Chryssie had appointed herself Taffy's caretaker. "That's t-rrific," said Jackie. "Unbelievable!" Until she died later that year, Taffy was the only *dog* I knew to have her own seeing eye dog.

But I don't want to get ahead of the story.

Of course, my big question that day was whether Jackie was going to the Inaugural and the answer was "yes." But she vowed she was not taking any camera to the Ball. She had a date with the Senator-elect for the Ball and by the hour of the dance he would have been sworn in and become a full-fledged Senator.

"I'll be out there taking pictures, or sketching, during the parade," she said, "and that will be enough pictures."

"You haven't helped me give up this madness of Christmas cards," I accused her. She had done a column asking people if they thought it was a good idea to stop sending Christmas greetings. Although they had all griped about that particular Christmas chore, not one person had wanted to discontinue that onerous, but charming, custom.

"Christmas cards are like the weather," Jackie said. "Everyone complains but nobody does anything about it."

"Well, if I'm as busy next year as I was this, I'll sign my name with a stitch on the sewing machine. It's the signing that takes the time."

"And looking up addresses," she added.

I asked about everyone at home, especially those little tykes, Janet and James, and found that Santa had been good to them and that, more important, they had been "good" to other people, making presents for them with their own little hands.

"Jackie," I said, "without your column I'd never have found out about the potato."

"Nor I," she agreed and we laughed. We recalled that a few days before Christmas, Jackie roamed the downtown department store toylands, stopping little children to ask if they thought Santa would come to their house Christmas Eve. One little girl said, "If you're good Santa leaves an orange in your stocking and if you're bad he leaves a potato."

"I learned something else, too," Jackie said. "Why the reindeer don't come along down the chimney—'they're too fat.'"

"But don't forget," I added, "'they stay put up there because if they run away Santa spanks them.'"

It had been a wonderful column and I had clipped it. Jackie had brought out the most imaginative streak in every child. I had marveled at the grave reasoning of children and, though I had two of my own, the answers when Jackie edited them seemed even funnier than the ones I could remember about Sylvia and Jimi. I had loved the logic of one little girl who had been warned that Santa wouldn't come if she bit her nails but had confided to Jackie that she wasn't worried.

"He can't watch so many children bite their nails," she had said, feeling safe to keep on biting.

Jackie confessed that her first poem, at age eight, had been an ode to Santa Claus. "It had a lot of winter spirit in it, too, and showed how a town looked in the holiday season," she said.

That reminded me that I, too, had once penned a free verse description of a wintry town for my newspaper column. I hauled it out and showed it to Jackie. *Port Gibson on a Cold Moonlight Night* was the title, and it just rambled along describing, nostalgically, what I saw on a walk.

Eventually we got back to Janet and James, whom she had just interviewed for the second time in their lives. We talked about how their answers revealed the difference in their personalities. I could see what Jackie meant about Janet being a bossy type of big sister, just as Jackie had said *she* had been.

Jackie had asked them both how they felt about going back to school after Christmas vacation. James had been bubbly and full of love for all the world, just as Caroline Lee had been at his age. "Oh, I'm glad," he had said. "I like everybody there. Nobody is my best friend but everybody is my friend. I have to go back because we are learning to read. We have a new book. I can't tell you what it is because I have to look at the pictures to tell."

But Janet had answered bluntly, with the seven-year-old sophistication that, from all the things I'd been told, had been Jackie's, too. Janet's answer was: "Well, I don't feel at all nice because I don't think school is at all nice. Why do you have to go to school anyway? I hate reading most because then Amy starts thinking she's the boss after Miss Sorel says I can be the boss. She says, 'Janet, now were's going to have page 30, when I've already asked for page 29.'"

It was either during that visit, or during the next, that I pointed out to Jackie a story in a Sunday supplement, "Moving Day at the White House." Knowing her interest in everything pertaining to the White House, I thought she might get an inspiration for a column and she looked at it with pleasure.

Only eight years later I would be reading about *Jackie's* moving day at the White House.

In January of 1953, however, Jackie was more interested in the fact that the Senator-elect had rented a house in Georgetown. She asked if she could use my house to change clothes before dates. "Would you mind if I stopped in now and then to change clothes so I don't have to drive way out to Virginia?" she had asked.

"Heavens, Jackie," I scolded her. "You don't even have to ask. Help yourself anytime. Just go on upstairs and make yourself at home. You know the way."

I felt as warmly toward Jackie as to a younger sister. She might be "big sister" to the household of youngsters out in McLean, Virginia, but to me she was the younger sister I never had.

Yet I never presumed on our customer-dressmaker relationship to ask questions about her personal life. Even if I had, Jackie was not the kind you could pump. I had seen customers try it with Jackie and fail dismally. It was an Auchincloss-Bouvier trait. None of the three—mother or daughters—broadcast their personal affairs as some other customers did, and I respected them more for it.

I would hear all kinds of gossip: who was having trouble with her husband, who was straying from the marital fold, who was not speaking to whom. But I never heard any of this from Jackie or her mother. They were simply not interested in gossip.

But going back to Jackie's personal code, I asked her one time if she had ever been spanked, and she said she had been for being downright stubborn. One day, for no reason she could remember now, she had simply refused to speak to someone. After the spanking she still refused, so spanking was no good in her case. Though Jackie was a little shy and diffident at times, she was stubborn and always made up her own mind. No one could change it. Only after reasoning it out for herself would she consent to change.

The refusal to gossip or chitchat about their affairs made some people comment that Jackie, and Lee as well, were a bit stand-offish. But I admired this trait in their characters —this refusal to broadcast all the intimate details of their, or other people's, lives. They talked when there was something worthwhile or amusing to discuss. Jackie could be very warm and congenial, but she just couldn't be pushed or prodded or bullied or wheedled into talking when she didn't want to.

Hardly anyone knew—not even her co-workers on the *Times-Herald*—that she was interested in the Senator. One night she came during our dinner hour to pick up a dress she needed that evening. It was about six-thirty. Three or four other career girls were there also to pick up their clothes. I can picture her now, standing in a corner near the door, quietly waiting her turn. One of the other girls was impatient. "I'm in a big hurry. I have a big date." I thought, yes, but not with a Senator. Jackie and I looked at each other but said nothing.

She went to Senator Kennedy's new house on Inauguration night and nobody knew—except those few she wanted to have know—and the other guests, of course.

Then they all went to take a look at the proceedings at the Inaugural Ball. Jackie must have been exhausted. She had put in a full day covering the Inauguration and the parade, staying with her sketch pad until the last elephant had lumbered past the reviewing stand.

Her story had been entitled, "Picnic Lunches Help Crowd Wait for Inaugural Parade." And through her eyes I saw it all—how "the grandstands suddenly came to life at 7:30 A.M. when the first program sellers appeared." How next had come the people "clutching cameras and picnic lunches." And how finally the Rolls Royces deposited "women in saris and mustachioed Ambassadors."

One woman had confided to Jackie that she had come to view the Inaugural parade because, when she'd seen the wedding procession of Princess Elizabeth on TV, she'd felt "cheated." Through the eyes of Jackie I saw the "Ambassadors" from Hollywood, too—Clifton Webb and "Prince" Mike Romanoff, with whom she had talked. I had seen Mamie jumping up in the reviewing stand, throwing kisses to the West Point cadets, and waving and crying "Thank you very much" to a group of singers on the Indiana float who sang, "Mamie, the First Lady of our Land."

And through her eyes I'd seen that cowboy from Montana, Monte Montana, lasso the new President while the guards ran quickly to the Presidential box and the reporters and photographers broke through the lines to take pictures of it. And I saw the Governor of Kansas wave a big sunflower while the President bowed and bowed and raised both his arms in his characteristic gesture. When it was over, I had wandered with Jackie back around Lafayette Park and found a poor marcher "slumped at the base of a tree." He was from the Redman Drum Corps of California and he complained bitterly about the streets of Washington not being fit for marching.

Through Jackie's ears, I heard him grumble about cobblestones. "Cobblestones! It was cobblestones most of the way. There's nothing but cobblestones all down the middle of Pennsylvania Avenue."

Yes, she told all about the Inaugural Day, except the

funniest thing of all, which was what happened to her at
the dinner party the new Senator, John F. Kennedy, gave.
The cook, who had come to fix the dinner, had made a
horrible discovery—there was no stove in the kitchen. So,
at the last minute the guests had dined impromptu on
hamburgers.

I didn't see any pictures of Jackie and the Senator in
any of the papers I read. The attention was all on Mamie
Eisenhower and on how Charles of Elizabeth Arden's had
come from New York to dress her suddenly famous bangs,
and how, at the Ball, she wore a gown of peau de soie in
Mamie pink, a softer shade than the one Jackie preferred,
designed by Nettie Rosenstein. It had a tremendous skirt,
was sprinkled with literally thousands of rhinestones, and
her pink shoes and pink bag were sprinkled with rhinestones too. Around her throat she wore a triple-strand
choker of simulated pearls and baguette rhinestones. Her
earrings were clusters of eight small pearls and eight rhinestones around one large center pearl.

But the jewelry was not genuine. The big news of the
day, fashionwise, was that the First Lady, with her stamp
of approval, had given new prominence to costume
jewelry. The costume beads had been designed by Trifari.

Mamie Eisenhower had also given new life to the fad for
charm bracelets. She had one which her husband kept en-
larging to mark each important event in his or her event-
ful lives. Sometimes, I was to learn, Mamie wore two
charm bracelets separated by a wide solid one.

Sure enough, I was to see the "Mamie style" dresses
become the rage of Washington. Everything became bouffant, more bouffant and softer than ever. More frilly and
feminine. Shoes suddenly matched dresses and hats were
made of the same material as the dress and were big
fashion news.

And in the midst of it, as though on a quiet little island

of her own, stood Jacqueline with her own mode of dress. She refused to copy the First Lady and kept to crisp materials, working out her own styles. She wore no charm bracelets or chokers, no big skirts for daytime, no shoes that matched dresses and hats. In those days I never saw her in a hat.

"I'm trying to develop a certain clear-cut line," she said, ignoring the styles of the day and studying, instead, the suggestions of *Vogue* and the French fashion magazines.

Sometimes when we were leafing through a magazine I would point something out to her, saying that it would become her, but if it looked the least bit cluttered or "cute" or had more than one embellishment, she would say, "It just isn't me, Mrs. Rhea. It would be t-rrific on someone else, but it's not for me."

I must confess the thought entered my mind that it was a good thing Jackie hadn't become a designer, because with everyone wanting dresses like Mamie's, Jackie would have starved.

I remember how impressed I had been—and depressed, too—when, in answer to a question in Jackie's column on whom women dressed for, only one woman had said she dressed to enhance her own type. All the others admitted they were more interested when they went shopping in guessing what men liked or what would impress other women.

I noticed that the wife of only one Cabinet member had worn a sheath dress to the Inaugural Ball. That was Mrs. Arthur Summerfield, the wife of the Postmaster General. I thought of that elegantly simple dress of Mrs. Summerfield's eight years later when I saw Jacqueline's slimmest-of-slim sheath gowns for the 1961 Inaugural.

What amazed me most about the Inaugural Ball of 1961 was that most guests still had the Mamie Eisenhower look in their bouffant evening gowns. Jackie, in her starkly slim sheath, stood out in a class by herself.

Back in that winter season of 1953, Jackie was still developing her own individual look. Once in a while she would tell me that the Senator had thought something she wore was "t-rrific" and I would be as proud as Punch. But sometimes when I asked how he had liked a certain dress she would say with a smile, "I don't believe he noticed."

My impression was that the Senator, although he had grown up surrounded by clothes-conscious women, including a mother who frequently shopped in Paris, was not too clothes-conscious himself and that he simply liked the total effect of Jacqueline's clothes. And what he liked best of all was her way of expressing herself and her ability to make him laugh.

Jackie was using this ability to play a little game with him in the winter months, calculated to make him give her his views on life, women and the treatment thereof. I wished I knew what his comments were in answer to her provocative questions as I watched each day's column and tried to read into it some hidden message.

There was one in which she asked what people thought was the food of romance, and an unromantic, literal-minded butcher said, "Filet mignon."

There was one in which she quoted Noel Coward's comment: "Women are like gongs, they should be struck regularly. Do you agree?" One man said that Noel Coward sounded like "the kind of man who would hold the candle while his mother chops the wood," and said that any striking done should be "in the form of a medal glorifying women for putting up with the amateurish, juvenile nonsense of most men."

A second man quoted Balzac to Jackie, saying: "It is not the question of striking forcefully or often but of striking *'juste.'* Struck forcefully, they shatter, struck often, they become brassy. Struck regularly—ah, the tone."

And as spring crept around the corner, I chortled as she asked whether Irishmen make good lovers. She used a writer as her authority and said: "The Irish author, Seán O'Faoláin, claims that the Irish are deficient in the art of love. Do you agree?"

The answers tended to put Latins so far in the shade it was more like a blackout curtain. One man said that the Irish were such effective lovers that two Irishmen he knew and worked with, who couldn't even speak English yet, were already surrounded and pursued by women.

Someone else pointed out that half the movie actors were Irish and a girl said with absolute finality, "The Irish are the true lovers of the world. They are the most romantic of all races and the finest lovers of the world. The Latins are greatly overrated. They are professional lovers, but the Irishman loves from his heart. They're so sincere."

Then the girl added a touching line, "I've got a purpose for this madness, in case you didn't realize."

I thought to myself, and so does a certain girl I know.

CHAPTER 11

THE YEAR OF THE BIG SPRING

SPRING HAD COME again to 1820 35th Street—dogwood blossoms and all—the most memorable spring I had known and the like of which I would never know again.

The days were bright and the sounds were sweet and we kept the French doors of the ground-level sewing room open onto the patio garden so as not to miss a single whiff or tweet. The colors on the rack behind me, when some of Jackie's and Lee's clothes were hanging there, formed an indoor garden of gay colors. For spring came early to Jackie that year. Even the sound of her voice, when she'd call home and say, "Hello, Mummy, what's the latest?" sounded full of suppressed excitement and anticipation.

And spring came early to her sister, too. For Caroline Lee was getting married.

Lee had followed in her big sister's footsteps and had been picked, in 1950, as the leading debutante of New York City, where she had been presented to society at the Junior Assembly.

But suddenly the little sister had taken the lead and

was first to the altar. The date was set for Saturday, April 18, 1953, and I received an invitation. I was thrilled that Mrs. Auchincloss had included me but I carefully avoided affairs of this kind which would make me look like a social climber.

Jacqueline came in with her sister when Lee ordered some things for her honeymoon in the Virgin Islands. And as I sewed the casual dresses and playtime togs for honeymooning in the sun I thought of how different the sisters were in their attitude toward clothes. Lee seemed to like many different types of dresses, whereas Jackie seemed to stick to certain basic styles and evolved her fashion changes slowly. One style grew out of another in a kind of progression which strove toward a goal which was the expression of her own personality.

If Jackie liked a dress she had it made up in several materials with only slight variations. Lee's clothes, on the other hand, were wonderfully colorful and varied, but did not show the continuity Jackie's did.

Lee was more dramatic in using striking contrasts, bolder fashions, more extreme lines. She was fundamentally more interested in clothes than Jackie was, and changed her styles more often. In my opinion, Lee always dressed in "high" fashion and is still more striking today in her dress than Jackie is.

I recall the dresses Jackie, as First Lady, and Lee, as Princess Radziwill, wore at the ballet in New York in March of 1961. Jackie wore a pale blue brocade cocktail dress she had worn before in Washington. Lee wore brilliant red, cut quite deep in the back. Lee's features are not sharper than Jackie's but sometimes give that impression because her hair has always been worn straight and fairly close to her face, giving the effect of dramatic wings. In contrast, Jackie has always given a less theatrical and more subdued appearance of elegance.

MR. AND MRS. HUGH DUDLEY AUCHINCLOSS

REQUEST THE HONOUR OF YOUR PRESENCE

AT THE MARRIAGE OF MRS. AUCHINCLOSS' DAUGHTER

CAROLINE LEE BOUVIER

TO

MR. MICHAEL TEMPLE CANFIELD

ON SATURDAY, THE EIGHTEENTH OF APRIL

AT HALF AFTER THREE O'CLOCK

HOLY TRINITY CHURCH

3514 O STREET

IN THE CITY OF WASHINGTON

When Caroline Lee carried yellow and white flowers at her wedding at the Holy Trinity Church in Georgetown, I was not surprised because yellow, a color which Jacqueline did not wear at that time, was Lee's favorite of the moment.

Her father, Jack Bouvier, gave the bride away to Michael Temple Canfield, who was connected with Harper and Brothers, publishers in New York. I thought of how the literary field was closing in on Mrs. Auchincloss. First her daughter Jackie had become a writer and now her daughter Lee was marrying into the publishing world.

The wedding was a family affair. Mrs. Auchincloss enjoyed the pageantry of the ceremony with Jackie in the role of maid of honor, Nina as bridesmaid and "Miss Janet Jennings Auchincloss" and "Master James Lee Auchincloss" as proud and very helpful attendants.

I learned that this was not the first time Master Auchincloss had been caught up in the social whirl. Mrs. Auchincloss told me, with relish, what had happened as a result of Jamie and Jacqueline sharing honors on one big day when Jamie was being christened and Jackie was having one of her coming-out parties. Both their names were engraved on the invitations and friends were invited to come to meet both. Soon after, *Mr.* James Auchincloss had received a return invitation—to a dinner dance. Since he was only six months old, he was forced to decline, but Jamie's early social success became a standing joke in the Auchincloss family.

After Lee's wedding, customers were beginning to say to me that they wondered if Jacqueline's career meant more to her than marriage. But Jacqueline said nothing.

I said nothing either, and watched Jackie come in more and more frequently to change clothes before a date. Something new had been added—she now brought along a little make-up case which she kept in the car. I think it had room enough for her daytime dress when she sloughed off her working clothes to emerge like Cinderella for the night.

I once asked Jackie what the Senator called her and she said, "Jackie, just like everyone else does. Nobody calls me by my real name, Jacqueline," and she pronounced it for me with the soft "J" and the ending "leen."

I thought:

Jacqu—leen
It rhymes with queen.

I was so busy that spring I hardly had time to walk the dogs or inspect my dogwood tree, which was making a special effort to increase its yield of blossoms. But I always took time to read Jackie's column in the *Times-Herald*.

Three days after Lee's marriage, Jackie was having an important interview. She was on Capitol Hill asking Senator John F. Kennedy what he thought of the Senate pages. His answer was delightful: "I've often thought that the country might be better off if we Senators and pages traded jobs. If such legislation is ever enacted, I'll be glad to hand over the reins to Jerry Hoobler. . . . I've often mistaken Jerry for a Senator. . . ."

Jackie promptly sought out the page, Jerry Hoobler, and asked him what he thought of the Senator. Jerry's answer was equally delightful: "Senator Kennedy is always being mistaken for a tourist by the cops because he looks so young. The other day he wanted to use the special phones and they told him, 'Sorry, mister, but these are reserved for Senators.' "

When Jackie's column appeared in the *Times-Herald* that day it was a "double header," with Senator Kennedy's comments in one column and Jerry Hoobler's directly opposite. As fate would have it, the Senator's future adversary, Richard Milhous Nixon, was also interviewed in that column with a corresponding comment from his favorite page.

I learned that Jackie had more material than she had written into the column. When I complimented her on it, she told me about the Senator having a terrible time using the little Senate subway. The guards, misled by his boyishness, were telling him to "stand aside and let the Senators on first."

"I didn't want to make it look too bad for him," she said. "I took pity on him."

What impressed me most in the case of the boyish Senator was that, according to reports, he hadn't pushed his way onto the subway but had stood aside and let the older Senators get on first, in order not to embarrass the operators.

This one thing alone made the Senator "a nice guy" in my book and probably someone worthy of the gentle Jacqueline.

Jackie, too, would not hurt anyone's feelings if she could possibly avoid it. When she would leave my place, I would see her little black convertible overflowing with the boys from Gordon Junior High across the street, who were waiting for her. She would chat with them gaily a few minutes and not just order them out. Sometimes this meant losing precious time in her busy schedule, because the boys were not anxious to let her go. But she always got away without being irritable or nasty or pulling her weight.

Jackie seemed very gay that spring and she was thinking more about clothes. I took this to mean that she was courting "Senatorial favor."

I can see her now, loaded down with camera, magazines and packages of materials—no hat, no gloves, hair flying in a short feather cut . . . a lovely tousled look. She would lay her things on the sofa to the right of the door. This was a big sectional sofa, covered in green, which went well with my green rug. A big, blond wood step table in the corner separated the two sections. The rug was my one folly and Jackie would kid me about it. That was because it was of a material which, if you dropped pins on it, would engulf them forever. It held pins like a sponge holds water and an octopus holds a sponge. I used to live in terror lest those of my customers who were always taking off their shoes to ease their feet would die of blood poisoning.

Jackie would laugh. "If you dropped a pin here, you couldn't find it unless you stepped on it in bare feet."

Jackie never took off her shoes. That was because she never wore uncomfortable shoes. Even when I saw her dressed for an evening date, the heels were only medium high.

"How do you manage to fit people all day and run up and down in those high heels you wear?" she would ask me.

"I've just gotten used to them, and if I changed to low heels I'd probably trip on the stairs or fall flat on my face."

"I think it's wonderful you can do it," she marvelled. "You're one of the quickest fitters I've ever known. It's so refreshing not to have to stand for hours."

But she was considerate about giving me time enough to do a job properly. "Do you think I could possibly have this one for the week end?" she asked. "The other things can wait until next week." With that kind of approach I would work faster and more conscientiously to accommodate her.

Jackie showed interest in my work and I was certainly interested in hers. I'd ask her if she had had a busy day. "No need to ask if it was interesting," I once added, "because I see by the paper it was."

She said, "Well, I just came from Capitol Hill and the nation is safe for another day."

I certainly enjoyed the new impression I got of Congressmen through Jackie's eyes—not pompous legislators, but very human and sometimes extremely modest individuals. I'll never forget the anecdote she told concerning a Senator, Wallace F. Bennett of Utah. He had thought someone was yelling at *him* when one page called to another, "Go get Senator Goldwater. He's wanted on the phone."

As Jackie put it, "Senator Bennett was seen hurrying all over the Senate floor and through the lobbies looking for Goldwater and trying to deliver the message."

That spring Jacqueline had me make a silk faille dress for afternoon wear. It was navy blue, made along very simple lines, with three-quarter length sleeves and lined in blue China silk. It had a higher neckline than I usually made for her and a soft bow at the neck, which was a little unusual for her, but very becoming.

It had a slim skirt, which she had me taper in from just below the hip line to the hem. This made the dress a standout from the monotony of wide-skirted dresses so in vogue at that time, and it made the wearer look very straight and slim. The round neckline did not stand away from her neck as most of her present ones do. And that is why she broke the line with the small bow. It started as a narrow band at the back of the neck and became a bit wider, ending in two pieces in front, which she tied in a bow, leaving the ends to come about three inches below the knot. It was like a coat dress, but the self-covered buttons stopped just before the hemline, and the front seam was sewn shut there to keep the line across the bottom unbroken by a gaping opening.

This dress, so simple but smart looking, tempted me to copy it for myself for a tea at the Western High School, where my claim to fame was that I was Sylvia's mother. I made the dress in pink shantung, a good color for me as well as Jackie, as I was extremely thin and had dark hair.

During the fittings of this blue faille dress, Jackie and I had another interesting conversation about color. She had just read an article describing what color does to the personality. A color a person disliked intensely, the article said, could give that person a feeling of insecurity or even of inferiority. A dull blue could give some women a feeling of depression while it gave others the happy feeling of spring showers.

"When I see a dull bullet blue, I want to shoot myself," I said. "And red makes me feel all's well with the world." Jackie said she liked pale blue, but that it was pink which made her feel that "June was busting out all over." Certain shades of green jarred miserably on her nerves. I told her I hoped the tone of my green rug wasn't one of them and she protested it wasn't. I finished off the subject of green by saying that I felt more people hated green than would admit it.

We decided that, perhaps, instead of a woman going out to buy a new hat to cheer herself up, it might be cheaper if she bought a scarf of some color that made her feel happy and gay.

Well, I thought, that was one way of getting out of buying hats.

At this time some of Jackie's questions in her column had a frankly romantic slant. And suddenly Jackie was asking a million questions about the married state. She went to a cooking class and asked what cooking tips the ladies would give a bride. I don't know how much use Jackie made of these tips, but I learned of a wonderfully simple dessert that is guaranteed to please husbands and children and takes only a moment to throw together. I clipped it from her column and have used it over and over.

Here it is: Combine a can of shredded pineapple, a tablespoon of lime juice and a half pound of cut up marshmallows and put on ice until chilled. Then, just before serving, whip a cup of heavy cream, season it with two tablespoons of sugar and fold into the pineapple mixture. Presto, dessert is served.

Another day she quoted Winston Churchill—of all persons—and asked if people agreed with him that, for a happier marriage, each member should have breakfast alone.

I remember she quoted Stendhal, the French novelist, in another column concerning how to "fall *out* of love," and in still another column she even asked other young women whether they thought girls should live with their families until they married or should get their own apartments. It made me wonder if she was thinking of striking out for greater independence.

But the question I clipped from the *Times-Herald* which amused me most that halcyon spring was based on whether people were glad they had married. "How do you feel about your spouse now?" she went around asking.

Lo and behold, in all six answers, everyone thought marriage was the greatest! Not a sour grape in the whole column. One man told how he and his wife had been married fifty-one years. They had eleven children, thirty-five grandchildren and eleven great-grandchildren. He recalled that his bride had weighed only ninety-eight pounds, but that marriage had so agreed with her she eventually got up to one hundred and fifty-five. And they were supremely happy.

Another man said he'd married the "best girl in the world" and he wouldn't trade places with anyone. "She's put up with me for seventeen years."

And the women were throwing bouquets all over the place, too. One said, "Oh, this is the opportunity of a lifetime. This is wonderful." She meant getting a chance to sing her husband's praises in public. They'd been married twenty-seven years "and married life gets better every year." She confessed she was at a loss for words to tell how wonderful life was. "When you love your husband that's all that matters," she said. "You love him more every year."

The others were equally delighted with the marital state and only one woman admitted that the first three years had not been perfect. She said she had lost her temper quickly in those days, but had conquered it. As for her husband, he was "cool as a cucumber and still very romantic." And he'd gotten her a flower for Easter. She could ask for no more.

Ah, I thought, as I looked out my sewing room door into the spring-flowered patio, love is grand and it's good to be alive, even as a spectator to someone else's lively romance.

Jacqueline Bouvier   Washington Times-Herald

Beware of Professional Gamblers

CHAPTER 12

SHE'S OFF TO LONDON
TO VISIT THE QUEEN

THE STAR ATTRACTION in my fitting room that wonderful spring was Chryssie, who not only was Taffy's Seeing Eye dog, but had also become the world's greatest dog sitter. She loved most of our visiting dogs except for a few—which she hated. At the top of her hate list was a French poodle. Chryssie was no snob or truckler to social position. In spite of the fact that the poodle's mistress was very prominent on the society pages, Chryssie wanted to throw the foppish beast out. So every time the clipped and manicured poodle was there, both dogs had to be tied to different doors, where they would sit and glare at each other.

Just like a woman, Chryssie fell in love and mooned around a totally unsuitable paramour—a collie about six times her size, named Peter. But her very favorite playmate was a white toy poodle named Gay Baby. It belonged to Jimma Strong. These dogs would wrestle and tumble all over the living room and they enjoyed themselves so much that sometimes Jimma and I would have to wait a while after the fitting was finished, because we didn't have the heart to break up this tumultuous play.

Mrs. Ellery Husted had a black-and-white spaniel which had one litter after the other. I remember that Jackie would ask Mrs. Husted how many puppies the dog had had this time, and it would be some tremendous number. Someone, seeing me picking up huge amounts of the dog's white hairs from my dark green rug, made a little joke about the dog's hair being as loose as its morals, and the joke, with embellishments, made the rounds.

Little Chryssie could be a heroine, too. I was fitting a teen-age customer who had brought along her large German shepherd, Frieda, which had been trained for years as her watchdog. This huge dog mistook my motives when I was fitting young Deedee Donahue, the granddaughter of the well-known financial writer, U. V. Wilcox. When she growled and started to come at me, Chryssie took in the situation at a glance, squeaked her loudest and attacked Frieda. What a scene that was! When we'd separated them, Deedee and I laughed so we could hardly stand up.

With so many dogs around, Jackie mentioned that out in Merrywood she and the other girls had each had a dog, making four dogs in all. I was amused to note that the Bouvier dogs had had typically French names, while the Auchincloss girls had given their dogs typically American names.

One thing that endeared Jacqueline to me was that she was one of the few customers who seemed to realize how hectic my life was and would say, "I hope you haven't been working too hard." I had, I reflected as I came up from down under with a heavy pile of clothes, but I wouldn't admit it. Still, it was nice to have someone show such interest.

If anyone had asked me what qualities made up a nice

person, I'd say kindness, tact and sympathetic interest in others—just what Jacqueline Bouvier always had.

Some other customers would toot their horns and I would have to run out into the street with their dresses, but never Jackie. If she were in an extreme hurry, she'd dash to the door and I'd hand them to her. She'd call "Thanks a million" over her shoulder and would be off in a flash. Jackie was *never* too hurried to be polite. Sometimes she would say, "I saw Mrs. So-and-So at the club dance and I loved her gown. I wondered if it was yours."

Jackie had a special interest in health problems, too. Not her own, but those of the Senator. He had picked up malaria during the War in the Pacific and suffered recurrences, and he had had trouble with his back ever since college days. I used to reflect that this brought out the maternal trait in Jackie—the Senator not only *looked* as though he needed care, he *needed* it.

And from what I could read in Jackie's column and between the lines of it, the Senator wasn't much interested in looking after himself. The page, Jerry Hoobler, had reported that Kennedy didn't even take time for a proper luncheon, just brought along a sandwich in a paper bag.

I never told Jackie how some of her material had nearly been ruined by teen-age boys in the neighborhood who had slipped into my sewing room downstairs one night and, as a prank, had proceeded to design a dress on the form standing there. They had combined some imported material of Jackie's with that of another customer and had cut here and there and pinned the material on the form.

I almost fainted when I saw their handiwork. I held my breath while examining to see if the material was ruined, but I managed to cut the cloth so that I didn't have to confess what had happened. I would have hated to admit that my shop had not been "secure" enough to protect the lovely and expensive materials left in my care.

I used to wonder why Jackie, with her perfect size ten, bothered to have any simple daytime dresses made for herself and didn't just buy them all ready-made, and then I realized that part of the reason was that it was hard to find dresses that were as utterly simple and pure of line as she wanted.

Ready-made dresses tended to have an overstated look and she definitely wanted understatement. She had a perfect horror of overdressing and, consequently, she was already one of the most elegantly dressed young women to come through my door.

Other customers sometimes came in with open-toed shoes, dangling earrings, bracelets, necklaces and pins— many pieces of jewelry at the same time. Jackie never wore open-toed shoes, day or night, but only pumps with medium high heels. Mrs. Auchincloss also wore this same type of shoe. Jackie never wore dangling earrings, only pearl buttons. Her necklace, when she wore one—was usually a single or double strand of pearls. Very rarely did she wear colored beads. And if she wore a brooch, she left off the necklace. If she wore a bracelet, it was never a charm bracelet, but a simple circlet of gold. And if she wore a bracelet, she left off other jewelry, except earrings.

The most important aspect of Jackie's style was that she had a sense of fitness about matching the dress to the occasion. This, to my mind, is true elegance. She might wear an extreme, strapless gown in the evening, but in the daytime she was ultra conservative in a shirtwaist dress with three-quarter length sleeves. She did not wear playtime dresses for street wear, but kept them for the country and the beach. She preferred solid colors to prints and seldom wore sharp contrasts.

Of course I wanted my daughters to develop their individual styles, but if they had to copy someone at this stage of their development, I was glad when they had the good taste to copy Jackie.

It was this spring that I noticed Jackie was not too concerned about nipping in the waist. I remember a black Italian silk suit I was working on. I made it up with a plain straight skirt with a small band at the top of the skirt, and put a series of small darts at the waistline to give the skirt more ease, instead of giving it a fitted look. The French use these small darts at the waistline frequently. The jacket was beginning to show Jackie's thinking toward a more relaxed look. It leaned toward the shorter length and was only semi-fitted at the waist, with three-quarter length sleeves. It had a small turn-back collar and small lapels. The buttons were of black bone and the buttonholes were bound.

Then there was a dress I made that spring which could fit into her wardrobe today as far as design is concerned. It was of filmy material—the only time I worked on any such lightweight material for her. It had a real "Jackie look," but the dress was flowered, and the dress which has become known as the "Jackie look" dress is of solid colored material.

But to get back to the dress, the material had come from Europe and the background color was white, which was covered with an all-over pattern of lovely pink flowers touched with muted green foliage.

I fashioned the dress in a semi-princess style, collarless and sleeveless and with gores in the skirt. The neckline was wide and round, but did not dip down low. It came down in back just as far as it did in front and the zipper in back extended about four or five inches below the waistline. The dress fell easily over the waist instead of being nipped in. The shoulder line extended just slightly beyond the shoulder bone, covering it.

This gown needed no trimming because of the beauty

of the print—in fact, trimming would have ruined it. The material was some kind of synthetic, but it was so gossamer-like that when I was working on it I felt I was attempting to put stitches in a cloud or a cobweb.

Suddenly, Jackie needed these costumes in a hurry.

She came *really* bursting in one day with the news that she was "off to London to visit the Queen." She had only a few days to get ready. She was thrilled and excited because she would be covering the Coronation of Elizabeth II for her newspaper. "I'll get a chance to do some regular writing," she said. She was going with several girls and was travelling on the *S.S. United States*.

"Will you take your camera and get some pictures?" I asked.

"Yes, I'm supposed to carry on my inquiring camera girl stories, but I just may throw my camera overboard."

I could see that Jacqueline was making this her real challenge to emerge as a writer, as well as a cataloguer of other people's comments. I asked what would happen to her column while she was gone and she said that, fortunately, she had done some in advance and was rushing to get more.

"I'm all set, except that I have to have something to wear."

I learned from some of my other customers that the newspaper was not financing her trip. She was staking herself to it, but the *Times-Herald* had been happy to give her the assignment to cover the Coronation, along with its veteran correspondents, as long as the cost would not be greater than they were regularly paying her. But they had upped her salary. She had just been promoted—every week her pay envelope contained the astronomical amount of fifty-six dollars and some cents. Well, the paper certainly got its money's worth because some days it carried two of her by-lines—one from London and one from Washington.

I noticed that before she left she went about gathering the American public's opinion on a few interesting matters. For one thing she asked, "Would you like to see the European custom of kissing ladies' hands started here?"

I thought the women she interviewed would say they adored it, but strangely enough they said they would be uncomfortable having their hands kissed, and not a man was for it. I laughed aloud when I read that one man wondered if the man is supposed to make a noise when he kisses a hand or is just supposed to be "silent about it."

I liked one man's answer concerning his approach to women. "I like to grab them and give them a big hug and anything short of that I wouldn't care for. It's too much effort for nothing."

Another burning issue of the day, which I was glad to see Jackie had tackled when I opened my *Times-Herald* one day, was whether people thought the Duke of Windsor, who had abdicated his throne, should attend the Coronation, in view of the sentiment in Britain against his wife, the Duchess.

I was interested to learn that most people, like myself, felt the Royal Family and the British Government had been "harsh" in refusing to accept the Duchess, and that the Duke should, as one man put it, just go some place else and "enjoy himself playing golf."

More and more my customers were quoting Jackie, commenting on what she had said and adding their own views. I wondered what we would do without her to give us something to chuckle about.

But Jackie didn't have time to sit around and join the conversation. She was rushing around getting ready for the big event, so busy that after I'd been up almost all night for several nights trying to complete her clothes she hardly had time to try them on when she came for them.

"Be sure to bring back some of those British tweeds," I said as she gathered up her things.

"I'll try to, if the Queen lets me have enough time for shopping," she laughed. "After all, this is a matter of the Queen's business and she may just keep me too, too busy."

She used a British accent as she spoke.

"Toodle-oo and good luck," I called.

A two-line rhyme came to mind as I watched her go, so excited and happy about her assignment:

> She's quoted,
> She's promoted.

---◄{ CHAPTER 12½ }►---

SHE'S BEAUTIFUL, SHE'S ENGAGED—
SHE'S UNEMPLOYED

I CALL THIS Chapter 12½ because I frankly do not like the number "13." I'm superstitious. But so is almost everybody. I remember that when Jackie asked whether people were superstitious about the number "13" in her column I got the impression that maybe she, too, wasn't crazy about that number. And then, recently, I learned that at a luncheon at the White House for Senatorial wives, Jacqueline had simply omitted having a number "13" table. Therefore, there isn't an unlucky number here, either.

I watched the *Times-Herald* breathlessly, waiting for Jackie's first story on her "foreign assignment." And then on June 1, 1953, suddenly there it was, right on page 2 of the newspaper and datelined from shipboard.

It was illustrated, not with photos but, I was thrilled to see, with Jackie's own inimitable squiggle drawings.

It was typical of Jackie that, while others were writing about famous people on shipboard, *she* was writing about their somewhat less famous dogs—dogs like Trooper and

Dizzy, which belonged to the Duchess of Windsor, and a haughty dog named Thomas, a Cairn of the Duke's.

Others were reporting the grandiose plans of the notables who were going to the Coronation. She was relating how the Duke's valet spent more time with Thomas than with his master. And that there were fourteen dogs on the *S.S. United States,* and the price for a sea voyage for a dog was fifty dollars.

Jacqueline Bouvier   Washington Times-Herald

Dogs Have Their Day on Coronation Cruise

Pluto and Bijou at the Hydrant

She told of one dog which drank nothing but bottled Poland water from the ship's bar. And of a special fire hydrant which had been set up to give a homelike touch to the dogs' quarters, and to help them get their sea legs.

Jackie drew Bijou at the fire hydrant with his friend Pluto, a dachshund who was travelling with the Jock McLeans. Pluto and Bijou met every morning at the fire hydrant, Bijou with his owner and Pluto with his mistress' daughter, Barbara, age five, whom Pluto so loved that he cried every time she left him.

There were dogs of every size and shape and ancestry, from Ti Ti and Hi Chow, two Pekingese, to Rebel, a proud police dog, Penny, a Spitz, and Pixie, an unabashed mongrel.

There was Zuzu, a fancy Skye terrier, whose real name was Yul de Mondane and who was not interested in coronations because he was on his way to the French dog shows.

Bijou was a French poodle, whose mistress confided to Jackie, "He adores France—not Paris, but the French countryside."

There were dogs with other problems. Bridget and Leo, a couple of English cockers, who were on their way to their estate near Salzburg, Austria, with their owners, former Ambassador to Canada and Mrs. Stanley Woodward, looked so much like foxes their very lives were in danger. Mrs. Woodward told Jackie, "We'll have to alert the landowners. They'll take them for red foxes and I'm so afraid they'll get shot."

When I saw this delightful "doggerel," I got out the column she had written earlier in Washington—the interview at the veterinarian's. I thought she was right! I finally had to agree. She should be a writer and not a dress designer.

On a separate page appeared her usual by-line column in which the question was: "Do you think Nathan Leopold should have been paroled?" Four out of six answered they felt he had paid his debt to society and should be paroled.

The next day the headline of her story was: "Crowds of Americans Fill Bright Pretty London."

"Oh to be in London, now that Coronation's here," said Jacqueline Bouvier in her lead, adding that Robert Browning would have forgotten all about England in April had he been in London at the time of the June Coronation.

I felt that I really had a ringside seat at the unfolding of an historic pageant. I watched the excitement of London through Jackie's eyes. I "watched" Jackie as it took her forty-five minutes to cross Trafalgar Square, instead of the usual three minutes. I saw the pictures of the Queen pasted in the front windows of all the homes and everyone out in their car to gaze at the multicolored bunting waving from the street lights and buildings.

What I especially liked was the way Jackie could make you see the people she was writing about by the use of their own idiosyncracies of speech—the mark of a good writer. A cabby told her, "Everybody's out in 'is car taking a peek at the decorations and them what 'asn't got a car is walking. Everybody's so good-natured I was telling my missus we should 'ave something like this every year."

Then a lady in waiting at Buckingham Palace, with typical British understatement, said, "Her Majesty gave each of us a piece of stuff for our gowns, which was rather nice." The description of the "stuff" which followed proved it had been closer to "wonderful" or "t-rrific" than "rather nice." The lady added, "Things have been in such an awful rush lately. So many fittings, things and such."

Jackie wondered, in print, if the Queen would change after the Coronation. She quoted a friend of the Royal Family, who told her that another monarch, King George V, "changed completely" from the fun-loving playboy of his Prince of Wales days, after he was crowned. "The ceremony has tremendous religious significance, you know," the friend explained to Jacqueline. "When the oil is applied by the Archbishop of Canterbury, that means you are God's anointed."

Eventually people would be wondering the same thing about Jacqueline—would she change when she gained the "title" of First Lady?

Good reporter Jackie ferreted out the "secret" that a hidden mark had been placed on the crown so that it wouldn't be put on backwards, as it had been in 1937 when the Queen's father, George VI, was submitted to the indignity of a backward crown.

I was interested to see that Princess Margaret was also in the news, making headlines quite different from her sister's. One day the papers proclaimed that she was involved in a "deep friendship" with Robin McEwen, a socialite attorney, and the next day they blared forth the news: "Divorced Ace and Princess Meg in Love," with a big picture of Captain Peter Townsend.

Meanwhile, back in Jackie's regular column in the U.S.A., Jackie was asking, "Do you think Aly Khan and Gene Tierney will get married?" The women proved themselves smarter because they bet they would not marry, and the men bet they would.

The day before the Coronation Jacqueline circulated among the crowds at Piccadilly Circus asking, "What has been your greatest Coronation thrill?" With typical Jackie luck, she found a man who had just put up the decoration of "a big glorious crown" on the Britannic Insurance Building and was as excited and proud of his feat as if he'd handled the entire Coronation ceremony himself.

One couple was thrilled by the prospect of sleeping on the curb all night in order to have a ringside—or "curbside"—seat next day.

Meanwhile, back on the back pages of the *Times-Herald,* Jackie had planted a question that was sure to interest a certain Senator—"What is your candid opinion of marriage?" I laughed when I read it and wondered, as I had several times before, how many people she had interviewed and photographed before finding three men and three women who were all in favor of marriage. A man with six children said, "A married man gets more respect from the world."

A woman said she recommended marriage because "people who have gone through life unmarried seem so frustrated and unhappy." That was *touché,* I thought.

The closest Jackie came to a negative answer was from a woman who said it was a bad day to talk to her because she had just had a fight with her husband and "some days I'd like to set a bomb under him," but then she went on sweetly to take all the blame for all of their quarrels. She said she always started them and then had to go "crawling back to say, 'Honey, I'm sorry.'" Even this encouragement, backhanded though it was, was certainly an answer to urge any man to take the plunge.

On June 9 Jackie broke into print again in a story from London which began, "The Mesta fiesta—second only to the Coronation—was the show to see in London last week."

Jacqueline Bouvier   Washington Times-Herald

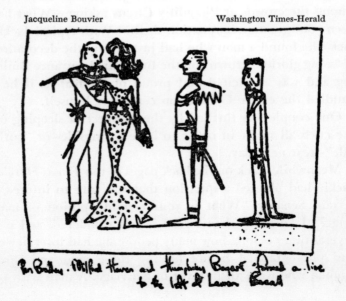

Jackie had attended the magnificent dinner ball given by Perle Mesta, former Minister to Luxembourg, in Londonderry House. As usual she told the off-beat bit about the party—how the Marquess of Milford-Haven had appeared in a colorful blue uniform with gold epaulettes and wearing a sword. He had asked a friend, "I say, do you think I'm a bit overdressed?" Jackie reported the answer was, "My Lord, I would say that you were." I made a mental note to ask her, when she returned, where the accent was on the "My Lord."

Her accompanying illustration was a delightful drawing of men standing in line to dance with Lauren Bacall—General Omar Bradley, Milford-Haven and Humphrey Bogart.

Everyone in my fitting room was full of praise for Jackie's wonderfully witty sketches of London scenes and agreed that she was doing the U.S.A. proud.

Suddenly Jacqueline's by-line was gone from the paper. The column was there, but someone else was doing it without a by-line. I wondered what was going on. I saw, above the "Mesta Fiesta" story, an editor's note that Jacqueline had gone to Paris for a few days to cover social life there. But I didn't see any more stories from her.

Later I learned that the Coronation was Jackie's swan song in newspaper work. I learned it from Jackie herself. She came in to say hello and to have a few things fixed. She was really happy—radiant, somehow.

Something was up, I could sense, and I was struggling to put my finger on it as I raved about her shipboard story and the "Mesta Fiesta" sketches. She told me bits about the trip and how, at the last minute, she had found a place to stay in crowded London.

We talked a little about the unique Coronation gown which Norman Hartnell had designed for Queen Elizabeth II. It had the emblems of all the nations of the

One hears a lot on the Promenade Deck

This Is London on Eve of Coronation

All the deposed monarchs are staying at Claridge's

Jacqueline Bouvier   Washington Times-Herald

British Commonwealth embroidered on its white satin material. The shamrock of Ireland in green silk, silver bullion and *diamanté*. India's lotus flower in mother-of-pearl, seed pearls and rhinestones. The thistle of Scotland in amethysts, *diamanté* and thread of silver bullion and green silk. The maple leaf of Canada executed in green silk, gold bullion and crystal. And how it had taken six girls two months to embroider the emblems—which also included Australia's wattle flower, New Zealand's fern, Ceylon's lotus, South Africa's protea flower, Wales' leek and Pakistan's wheat, cotton and jute blossoms—all clustered around the Tudor rose of England.

Then I saw what was different—a diamond and emerald ring on her engagement finger. Jackie wasn't the kind to hold out her hand and say, "Look, guess what?" She liked to wait until I had noticed something new. So it was this time. I noticed, as she knew I would.

"Well, does this ring mean what I think it means?" I asked.

"Yes, it does."

"Let me look at it."

She held her hand out proudly. "This time this is *it*," she said.

She told me how happy she was and how life had new meaning. I told her I was happy too, but I hoped it wouldn't mean that I would see less of her.

"I'm sure it won't, Mrs. Rhea. I'll be here more than ever."

"Do you know yet what your plans are?" I asked.

"No, not definitely, but I hope sometime this fall we'll be married. Please don't mention anything about my engagement until it is announced. I know you won't."

I was as pleased as if this was happening to a younger sister.

"How did it come about?" I asked. "Was it like that

column of yours in which the fellow was playing golf and his game was off so he decided his trouble was love and he went straight to the gal and proposed?"

Jackie laughed. "Something like that. He was there when the ship docked and he popped the question."

In my mind's eye, I could see the scene, as in a movie. He, a little nervous. The noise, the crowd, the excitement. Had he said, "Let's find a quiet place to talk"?

"The column," I exclaimed, suddenly remembering. "What's going to happen to the column?"

"Well, Jack says one writer in the family is enough. Actually, I've been getting a little tired of the same format all the time. There wasn't enough chance for real writing."

But I couldn't believe that Jackie was through and I would never see her by-line again. She'll write novels, I thought. Or maybe she'll do plays with lots of sparkling conversation. She'll surely be writing again. Maybe poetry. Maybe children's books.

Yet I could see that for her the column was now something in the past. Done and finished and time to move on. It gave me a feeling of unreality. I had lived with it so long, that I had, in effect, shared her life through it. I had discussed it with her and laughed about the trials of getting people to talk and the tribulations of rushing back to the office with a wonderful comment and then finding the accompanying picture was unusable and having to rush out and get another interview fast if the person had closed his eyes when she snapped the picture or she had forgotten to pull the slide.

Now she was saying with a happy smile, "I'm unemployed."

I smiled too, but I felt sad.

I didn't have long to wait for the engagement announcement or to look hard to find it. It hit the front page of the *Times-Herald* on June 25. I'll never forget the lead: "A story book romance between the *Times-Herald*'s Inquiring Camera Girl and the United State Senate's most eligible bachelor will culminate in marriage September 12 in Newport, Rhode Island."

It was the glowing account of how the town's prettiest inquiring photographer was marrying the "tall, tousled-haired Senator from Massachusetts" who had never lost an election. And it told all about Jackie's fine family background.

"Her maternal grandmother is the former Caroline Marslin Ewing of Philadelphia who for many years was honorary president of the New York Foundling Hospital, conducted by the Sisters of Charity of the New York Catholic Diocese," it commented. "She is related to the late Mother Katherine Drexel of Philadelphia, founder of the Order of the Blessed Sacrament."

Then it told how Jacqueline had made her debut in 1948 at Newport, the Junior Assembly in New York and the Autumn Ball in Tuxedo, New York.

I'll bet a lot of people who had been interviewed by Jacqueline were really staggered to learn that the pretty girl who questioned them and had acted just like any other girl was really an heiress and society luminary. Even a few of my customers who had seen her come and go commented that they hadn't realized who she really was.

Many customers who knew Jackie confessed they hadn't known she was going with Senator Kennedy. Even some of the reporters on her own paper said they hadn't known. They'd read her interview with the Senator and his page on Capitol Hill but, after all, she had interviewed a lot of other bachelors in her more than a year on the paper.

Her boss had kidded her about marrying a man twelve years older than she but, when I heard that, I reflected that her mother had been an even greater number of years younger than her father—fifteen or sixteen years.

Many people now surmised it had been a whirlwind courtship that had begun in April when she had interviewed him. But of course it had been going on for some time.

Almost everyone in my dressing room had some comment. Some thought Jack Kennedy was so handsome and exciting that they would give anything to change places with Jackie.

Some—the rock-ribbed Republicans—said it was a shame, with all the good Republicans in the world, that Jackie had to pick a dyed-in-the-wool Democrat. "It goes against all her family traditions."

Some commented on how strange it was that a fashion-conscious girl would pick a man with practically the worst fashion record on Capitol Hill. So little did he care about clothes, those who knew him told me, that he had been seen on occasion with socks that didn't match. And once his shirttail had been out hanging down under the back of his coat when he rose to speak in the hallowed Halls of Congress. And, horror of horrors, he sometimes permitted his dry cleaner to press a crease in the sleeves of his coats.

Crease or no crease, Jack Kennedy didn't seem to notice.

Then there was the matter of his ties, which some felt looked "like Christmas presents." "He just doesn't seem to care how he looks," said one customer to another. "Those wild ties and those wide-striped suits should be out."

"And he doesn't get his shoes shined," said another.

"How can he?" commented the first one again. "He never goes to the barber shop." The others laughed and she added, "You know what I mean, *he* hardly ever goes."

My customers got to talking about whether Jackie would change the Senator. "Don't worry," said one. "Just wait till the wedding, she'll have him straightened out in no time."

In my mind I disagreed, but I said nothing—after all, "the customer is always right." But I had a feeling Jacqueline wasn't going to take anybody in hand. And the reason I thought so was that she had done a column on this subject and had learned how men felt about their wives picking their suits and interfering in their choice of clothes. If the Senator changed, I decided, it would be through her example, not by pressure. Though the Senator was not dressing up especially well to please Jackie, she was certainly dressing up to please him, I thought, as she would come hurrying in to change her clothes at my place before a date.

Jackie was one person, I was sure, who was smart enough to benefit through the experiences of others. Every man, with only one exception, had told her that he deeply resented wifely help in picking clothes. The exception, too, was subject to challenge, because he was a clothing store owner who might have been looking at Jackie as a potential customer. And his reasoning had been spurious. He had said that a woman should pick out her husband's clothes "because she is the one who has to look at them more than the guy who wears them."

But the men who didn't own haberdasheries had been almost belligerent on the subject. One had said he would "definitely not" trust his wife to pick out his suits because she couldn't even pick out a necktie. Another had maintained that "women shouldn't even be *allowed* in men's clothing stores." He had gone on at length and with eloquence, ending disgustedly, "If they see a light blue satin tie with forget-me-nots on it, don't think they won't buy it."

No, I didn't expect to see the Senator change from a tousled-haired, casual dresser in the near future.

I reflected what good training Jackie's column had actually been for marriage. It was like a field course in psychology. Through her adroit questioning of people, she had really gotten to learn how people thought and reacted and what mistakes they had made in life and what they would do over if they could.

It wasn't just fun questions she had asked about life and love and marriage. She had asked serious ones too. She had asked people what they were living for—and had gotten a wonderful thought from former Arizona Senator Henry Fountain Ashhurst that "the chief business of man on earth is justice."

She asked whether engaged couples should reveal their pasts, which brought out good arguments on both sides. And again, she asked if married couples approved of joint bank accounts. And, "Would you postpone your marriage plans if you had to live with in-laws?"

She asked whether husbands and wives should criticize each other. And she had asked if people believe in spanking children and what changes they planned to make in the raising of their children from the way they had been brought up.

Yes, I thought the column had been good training.

Jackie might be out of a job now, but her future looked pretty rosy.

─◄{ CHAPTER 14 }►─

BEAUTY PARLORS, COUNTRY STORES AND DRESSMAKERS' FITTING ROOMS

MY SHOP was better than a party line for hearing what was going on in Washington's smart set. I don't know whether you hear more gossip in a beauty parlor, a country store or in a dressmaking establishment, but it must be a close tie. Some of my customers would try to pump me about what other customers said, did and were wearing. I had to be very careful, or I'd be known as the town's gossip and lose all my customers.

It wasn't surprising to me that they had often asked about Jackie Bouvier, because she was both society's darling and worked at a lowly newspaper job. I reflected that one week of her wages would scarcely pay for one of her dresses, but I never "reflected" aloud. I just talked about how I enjoyed reading her columns and speculated that maybe we would all some day be reading novels she had written.

"You have to start somewhere," I would say.

Some of Jackie's friends thought a newspaper office was

not a proper atmosphere for a girl brought up in polite society. Some thought she would end by marrying a reporter, and they were right. She did—a former one. He had covered the Potsdam Conference and other major events for *International News Service*.

But they weren't satisfied that the former reporter was now a Senator, because some of the old guard Washingtonians considered politics too rough-and-tumble for their exclusive set. They felt Jacqueline should marry someone whose life was devoted to culture, travel and maybe the world of finance. A banker or a broker would have suited them better than an energetic, hard-hitting Senator who, despite his father's wealth, acted as though he had pulled himself up by his bootstraps.

And he hadn't always gone easy on his own political party, either—or the man at the nation's helm. In his campaign for the Senate, John F. Kennedy had publicly demanded that President Truman call a special session of Congress to enact new price control laws, to fight the high cost of living. This came to my mind years later when ex-President Truman did not break his neck coming out for Kennedy for President or campaigning for him. Had Kennedy's demand in 1952 been the start of the dissension?

And speaking of dissension, the only dissension I knew of between Jackie and the Senator grew out of politics.

Sometimes she would be invited to a dinner party at his house and would be the only non-political person there. I heard from a friend that Kennedy would talk politics with his friends so animatedly and steadily that sometimes Jackie got a bit fed up and left for home while the evening was still young.

And sometimes she would merely leave the room to see if he would notice she was gone and come looking for her. He always did notice and would find her and bring her back. Sometimes she'd be in the hall, a little hurt and frustrated, waiting to be found.

Well, I thought, Jackie is smart enough to know if you can't lick 'em, join 'em. One of these days she'll become a master politician or the best listener at a political convention—a Democratic one.

The day after the anouncement of the engagement I noticed the by-line on the Inquiring Camera Girl column was Dale Chestnut. I wondered if the column would change her life as it had Jackie's.

I wondered how much the column actually had to do with Jackie getting engaged to a former fellow newspaper reporter. He had quipped to friends that he was marrying Jackie to "get rid of the competition."

I had a feeling the column had been very important in impressing the Senator that Jackie was not just another idle "society girl."

And just as Jackie had wanted a career that was purposeful she wanted a husband whose career was purposeful also. The Senator, from all I could gather, would never have picked a dress designer for a wife, just as Jackie couldn't bring herself to marry a man in the field of high finance.

Though Kennedy's occupation and preoccupation with politics sometimes frustrated and annoyed her, she respected him for his dedication in being the "Compleat Politician."

"I am fascinated by the way he thinks," she told me. "He summons every point to further his argument."

Both loved books and presented them to one another as gifts. It certainly wasn't an expensive courtship because Jackie would rather have books than anything else—even though some of the art books she collected cost over one hundred dollars apiece.

Once, possibly for the Senator's benefit, she asked the

members of the feminine sex if they agreed that "diamonds are a girl's best friend," and printed triumphantly the comment of a Falls Church housewife who said she had thought so until she married and had children, and that now she wouldn't trade her wonderful husband and children for all the diamonds in the world.

Jackie told me she couldn't agree more with the woman. "You can't talk to diamonds," she said. "They won't talk back."

But getting back to money, for some reason the Senator had more trouble with it than people who didn't have any. He was always forgetting to carry it. I guess he was so free of personal money worries he just dismissed money from his mind.

I don't know how many times Jackie had to cough up a coin for a parking meter or lend him the money for the dinner, but everyone talked about how he never had been able to remember to carry the green stuff.

In college he'd gone out on dates and after dinner found his pockets were as bare as old Mother Hubbard's cupboard. On Capitol Hill, a customer told me, he was just as bad and there were running gags about how Kennedy was saving money by spending his friends' and how "Kennedy should be put in charge of the United States budget."

One of the stories I heard most often was that the Senator's father, Joseph Kennedy, had given each of his children a million dollars. But from what I heard, Jackie didn't have to worry about money either because both her father and her step-father were exceedingly wealthy.

Once, when a customer wondered if Jacqueline was dazzled by the Senator's great wealth, another customer held that this was one marriage not influenced by money and said that Jacqueline, too, had come into money on her eighteenth birthday and was independently wealthy. Later

I heard someone put her personal wealth at a level with his original trust fund—one million dollars.

I wondered how it would feel not to have to worry about money. I had been trying to set some aside for my daughters' college educations and was finding it almost impossible. Besides, I was chafing at the bit. I hadn't had a vacation since I'd gone to work in January, 1947, except to go to the hospital, and that could hardly come under the category of fun.

I heard of an opportunity to go into the manufacture of dresses in Baltimore and I lined up a job to learn from the ground up, starting with the laying out of the commercial pattern, so I decided to make a change.

For several months that summer in '53 I became a commuter, keeping my business in Washington, working part time in Baltimore. It was, of course, impossible, and before the summer was over I shut up shop in Washington and moved to Baltimore bag and baggage—and mirror.

Before Jackie left for Newport, where she would be spending the summer now that she was an "unemployed" writer, I made her a few vacation things, overblouses to wear with shorts and slacks, and a few shorts and halter sets, but that was about all.

As I commuted, I thought how life had changed and how much I missed the column and being a reporter vicariously. Something definitely was gone from my life. But for Jackie's sake, I was so happy that she had found someone so suited to her. Both of them were writers. The Senator had even written a best selling book, *Why England Slept,* when his father was Ambassador to the Court of St. James and he was his father's aide.

Both had lived abroad. Both ignored their wealth and made their own way in the world, among people who were not equally affluent. Both kept their personal lives to themselves. I was glad Jackie had found someone who was as reticent about his personal life as she was. They could have had their pictures on the society pages practically every day of their courtship but, instead, they had preferred to meet quietly for dinner at the home of friends or at their own homes, or had slipped into a theater to see an occasional movie together.

The Senator would certainly fit in well with the Auchincloss clan. Even teen-age Nina said in her step-sister's column, "You are the slave of the spoken word. The unspoken word is your slave."

How well they had kept out of the limelight was illustrated, I thought, by the fact that just before the engagement was announced, the *Saturday Evening Post* had published a story about the eligible young bachelor Senator and it didn't even mention Jacqueline's name. As a matter of fact, while telling that he was considered the top catch in Washington, it failed to link him with any particular girl and, as its illustration, used a picture of him talking with the daughter of a former Ambassador.

Yes, they had certainly proven themselves alike in shunning personal publicity.

Another trait they shared was the modesty each had about the wealth and social position of their respective families. The story was told me that one of Jack's friends knew him for a long time before discovering Jack came from a distinguished family. Finally the friend asked if he were related to *the* Joseph Kennedy, whose achievements he started listing. Kennedy answered simply, "My father," and changed the subject.

Jackie, I was always surprised to see, bent over backwards to keep people from thinking she was anything other than a hard-working girl reporter who needed the salary. On the job she dressed more simply than many other newspaper women who were my customers.

Nor did Jackie ever boast of her education. When one

man she interviewed commented on her cultured speech and asked where she had been educated, she merely answered, "George Washington University," leaving out Vassar and the Sorbonne.

I'll never forget the way one of my customers gave her stamp of approval to Jackie's choice.

"It's all right for Jackie to marry Senator Kennedy," she said. "I looked it up."

"Looked it up?" I asked. "What do you mean?"

"Their horoscopes," she said. "Jackie was born in July— she's a Leo. For best results you are supposed to marry a person born two months before or two months after you. So that means she should marry a Gemini or a Libra. And that's what she's going to do. Jackie was born almost exactly two months later than the Senator. He is May 29— Gemini. She is July 28. Do you realize what this means? Her artistic ability and warmth and helpfulness—a Leo is always helpful to the man she loves—will be there to guide the Gemini and keep him sticking to his goal."

"I've got news for you," I said. "Jackie was not born two months later than the Senator."

My customer was shocked. "She wasn't?"

"No," I said, "she was born something like twelve years later than the Senator."

My customer was so mad she almost refused to tell me more about how this was a perfect match and Jackie would be an extremely dedicated wife. She would be patient with her husband who was ruled by the "nervous" sign of quicksilver, Mercury.

I thought, as I rode my weekly train, how this was, in effect, the second time lightning had struck my sewing shop.

One of my helpers was a Filipino girl who suddenly announced she was quitting to marry into the Royal Family of Siam, now Thailand. At the time I thought how such a thing could happen only in Washington, and that probably my little helper was the only one I'd ever meet who would become automatically famous through her marriage. But, of course, that was before Jackie. My helper brought her fiancé to meet me before they left for Thailand. I was thrilled for her. She would be a part of the diplomatic world from then on.

Jackie would be a part of the political world. I thought of how fortunate these girls were and how no one can know, in the gamble of life, who will be at the point of the arrow when the wheel of fortune spins to a stop.

At first I corresponded with Jackie—she was at the Auchincloss estate in Newport—and told her what I was doing. She was rather shocked that I was working in a factory but sympathetic to what I was trying to do.

The factory was exciting. I was fascinated to see how saving half an inch of material in a pattern can result in hundreds of dollars profit in mass production. The first day they finally let me lay out my first complete garment, I got everything in but one pocket. I spent the whole afternoon re-arranging the jigsaw puzzle until I got the pocket in the specified amount of material.

So when I heard that the Army saved $666,000 a year by eliminating the little watch pocket on the G.I. uniforms, I wasn't surprised. I also laid out ties for three days but found that too monotonous.

In one letter I asked Jackie if she'd like me to do any of the sewing for her trousseau. Her answer, on Hammersmith Farm stationery, was addressed to me at Baltimore.

I hadn't told Jackie yet I might not go back to Washington. I didn't know *what* to do. My health was not good and I had mentioned it to Jackie but I did not tell her that the doctor thought I might have to go to the hospital eventually for another operation. He also recommended that I slow down—stop running up and down stairs—and do easier work. In fact, he recommended I stick with my new Baltimore work and give up Washington.

I didn't want my daughters to worry about my health, so I had been trying to convince them a transfer to Baltimore would benefit me financially and would help me further their education, but they would have none of it. In fact, I almost didn't move because of them, so difficult did they make it—especially my younger one, who was now fourteen.

Recently, when my sister found out I was writing my memoirs, she sent me some of the letters I had written her during this dreadful time in the summer of 1953, which told how both the girls had refused to go to Baltimore even to see how they would like it and were staying with their friends in Washington. I had given grudging permission, to ease the tension while I figured things out, and tried to reason with them on my weekly trips back.

Meanwhile I was debating what to do about the invitation I had received to Jacqueline's wedding. How I cherished it!

I was also invited to the reception and I studied the little enclosed cards which accompanied the wedding invitation.

But the more pressing problem was what the girls and I should do.

I reached a decision to stay in Baltimore. Jackie had written many columns on the subject of bringing up children and one of the points, which had been made by a Juvenile Court judge, was that parents had to be the ones to make decisions and not be run by their children. A dangerous trend in our society was just that—parents were being run by their children. Well, I was being the captain of our little ship and I was praying that it would go well for us.

Mrs Mini Rhea.
4213 Parkton St.
Baltimore 29
Maryland

HAMMERSMITH FARM
NEWPORT, RHODE ISLAND

Dear Mrs Rhea —
I'm so sorry I couldn't answer
your letter sooner — things have been
in an awful rush.
You see I'm up in Newport now all

the time – & most of my trousseau I get in N.Y. by going to wholesale houses Then the rest of it I'll get this winter after I'm married –

I would have loved to have you make me some things – but we're both in the wrong cities!

I do hope you come back to Washington – I have loads of ideas whe– I get back there in January – I hope you have a good summer & that you're feeling better –

Love Jackie

MR. AND MRS. HUGH DUDLEY AUCHINCLOSS

REQUEST THE HONOUR OF YOUR PRESENCE

AT THE MARRIAGE OF MRS. AUCHINCLOSS DAUGHTER

JACQUELINE LEE BOUVIER

TO

THE HONORABLE JOHN FITZGERALD KENNEDY

UNITED STATES SENATE

ON SATURDAY, THE TWELFTH OF SEPTEMBER

AT ELEVEN O'CLOCK

SAINT MARY'S CHURCH

SPRING STREET

NEWPORT, RHODE ISLAND

I'll never forget how sorry, but understanding, my customers were. As I wrote my sister, "It really made me feel good to see how my customers felt about me leaving." And I told her how it felt finally to have had the courage to act decisively. "It's funny," I wrote, "how much better I feel now that I have made the break."

Now that I was acting with maturity, even Jimi resigned herself to the move and "decided" to come along.

But a funny farewell took place with the corner delicatessen man. He almost had tears in his eyes as he saw me go. "Your chauffeurs give good atmosphere to this place. Good class," he said. "And they eat so much when they are waiting. I hate to see you go."

There was someone else who hated to see my establishment close—a lonely boy who hung around watching. "You mean you're not going to do sewing any more?" he asked.

"Not here, anyway," I said. "I'm moving to Baltimore."

"Is somebody else going to do sewing here?" he persisted.

"Not that I know of," I said, wondering what in the world he was getting at.

"Oh," he said, dejectedly, "then Jackie won't be coming here either. The camera girl."

"I know who you mean," I said. "No, I don't believe she will be coming here."

"Gee," he said, starting to walk away. "I had a real good idea for her."

--⊰{ CHAPTER 15 }⊱--

TWO PATHS DIVERGE . . .

As Jacqueline's wedding drew near, the wheel of fortune spun my way. While at the factory, I had a side order for dresses of my own design. True, I was limited in scope because they were square dance costumes, but it looked like the beginning of my own designing business and I was thrilled.

But again I was faced with a big problem. If I went to the wedding, I couldn't get my first order filled. I *had* to make up my mind.

I decided to stick with the order, get the work out.

I have kicked myself ever since. The designing job did not last forever and I missed a thrilling moment of American history.

How I would have loved to have been there. People who had been lucky enough to go gave me all the details of the wedding, and I bought the papers that told me the most about it—the Washington *Times-Herald,* even though I was in Baltimore—and, for the first time, *The New York Times.*

I had heard that Jackie was spending a lot of time at the Kennedy estate at Hyannis Port, getting acquainted with the whole Kennedy clan, vigorously playing the rugged game of touch football and beachcombing with the Senator.

I had heard how Jackie and the Senator had gone to get the wedding license at the Newport City Hall in casual clothes and a photographer had caught them. The Senator had had to borrow a coat and tie to have a more dignified picture taken.

I had heard that Jackie and the Senator hadn't really wanted a big wedding, but only a small family affair in keeping with their quiet courtship—and from what Jackie told me I knew this to be so.

But with a girl as socially prominent as Jacqueline, and a Senator who had been voted by Hollywood columnists and reporters as the most eligible man in the whole country, even ahead of movie stars, as the main characters, a crowd was bound to congregate.

And they did. People came by the thousands to stand outside Saint Mary's Church in Newport. What a mob scene that was!

Some said the wedding was "just like the Coronation." Over six hundred prominent persons—members of Congress, diplomats and socialites—managed to squeeze into the church to watch the ceremony.

Whole busloads of sight-seers had descended on Newport to see the Senator take a bride. Jackie reacted to the adulation with surprise and a little fright, but the Senator took it in his stride and enjoyed every minute of it. Suddenly the girl who had been able to walk unattended down Washington streets, stopping people to take *their* pictures, had to be protected by the police from being crushed by the camera-clicking crowds.

I didn't blame her for being a little afraid. *The New*

York Times estimated that a crowd of three thousand broke through police lines and nearly crushed her when she left the church amidst rose petal confetti and rice. It said the wedding far surpassed the Astor-French wedding of 1934.

The wedding party and guests all piled into cars and formed a procession half a mile long for the drive to Hammersmith Farm. I cried a few tears into my sewing as I thought of how I could have been among them. I felt even worse when Mrs. Husted told me, later, that I could have gone with her.

I felt like a martyr until I heard that someone who had attended the wedding had suffered much more than I—and had suffered physically. That was the bridegroom. The Senator, I knew, had been hospitalized at George Washington Hospital for a recurrence of malaria several weeks after the engagement announcement and had recovered from it, but on the day of his wedding his back was giving him such trouble that kneeling at the altar had been torture.

Yet he had gone gamely ahead with the festivities at Hammersmith Farm and few had been aware of his misery. The guest list certainly brought back memories. Mr. and Mrs. Arthur Krock were there and it reminded me of how much they had influenced the lives of Jackie and the Senator and of me. I smiled as I reflected that the Krocks even used to help out the Senator when he entertained by lending him their butler, George. And after the marriage George became the Kennedys' full-time helper and today is with them at the White House.

Mr. and Mrs. Charles Bartlett were at the wedding and Mrs. Bartlett, who had seen the romance blossom from the moment they were introduced at her house, was an attendant at the ceremony. Mr. and Mrs. Bernard Gimbel were there and I thought of how I enjoyed shopping for supplies at their stores.

Caroline Lee Canfield was there, and, in fact, had come all the way from England, where she was now living with her husband, to be matron of honor.

I remembered the two Bouvier girls as carefree young women coming in together to have playtime clothes made. How quickly life gives us cares and responsibilities, I thought. Now I heard that Lee did not like having to live so far from her family and friends and was quite miserable. And Jacqueline would now have the responsibility of being hostess to her husband's political friends, and those of the opposing party, too, like Republican House Speaker Joseph W. Martin, who attended the wedding. I thought of what Jacqueline had stated as her ambition, as a schoolgirl, in her class yearbook. It was "Not to be a housewife." Now I heard she was already collecting recipes.

The thing I felt worst about was Jacqueline's wedding dress. I must say I was shocked when I saw pictures of that dress because it didn't look a bit like Jackie. It was not the sophisticated and elegant look that I had come to expect of her. It was the one time she was really out of character, although on a frilly type of girl it would have looked fine.

You may say that I was jealous because it was made by another little dressmaker, but I really don't think I was possessed by the green-eyed monster because I thoroughly approved of all the dresses later made for her by Oleg Cassini. They were all true to her personality. The wedding dress was, in my opinion, what Jackie had often said before of some dresses I had pointed out to her in the French magazines, "It's just not me."

The dress was made of fifty yards of ivory tissue silk taffeta, with a portrait neckline, a tight-fitting bodice and an excessively full skirt. It resembled, somewhat, Jackie's dress at her coming-out party in Newport. But the wedding dress had tremendous ruffles and circles of ruffles repeated all around the voluminous skirt. These almost endless ruffles were what I most objected to. I counted eleven rows of ruffles around the bottom of the dress and above them were large concentric circles of ruffles which diminished at the center, where there were sprays of flowers. There was also a spray of orange blossoms falling down one side of the skirt. The dress couldn't have been fancier. But I had the feeling that Jackie was trying to please everyone—to dress according to everyone's idea of a bride.

I would have loved to have seen Jackie use the heirloom veil of rosepoint lace as the feature attraction of the costume, rather than the eye drawn inexorably to the tremendous swirls on the skirt. I would have put Jacqueline in a plain white gown, undecorated except for the crowning glory of the veil which had been worn by her sister, her mother and her grandmother before her.

Her headdress of lace and orange blossoms and her bouquet of pink and white spray orchids would have been additional ornamentation enough. All those ruffles were not needed for someone as beautiful as Jacqueline.

Jamie and Janet were big stars at the wedding. Janet was the flower girl, dressed in a little gown which was an exact replica of those of the matron of honor and the bridesmaids, in pink silk with a strawberry-colored sash. And Jamie was the page, in an outfit he must have detested—velvet pants and white silk blouse with a big bow. He held Jacqueline's train, which was the end of the rosepoint veil.

I was not surprised that Jackie's wedding and reception had featured pink. It was her favorite color, and I remembered how, just a few months before, her sister Lee had built her wedding around the color yellow, which was *her* favorite.

The same day Jackie was married there was a fashion ad in *The New York Times:* "Fringe on a binge." For some reason that stuck in my mind for a long time—probably because of the rhyme. I remembered it again when, on her trip to Canada—her first to a foreign country as the First Lady—Jacqueline Kennedy wore a sensational evening gown which featured a row of fringe around the hem. I noticed, though, that Jackie did not let it go "on a binge" but kept it carefully neat and restrained.

I remember so many other things which made an imprint on my mind because they were in the news at the time of the big event which I missed. At about the same time, Dick Haymes and Rita Hayworth were getting married.

And the very day after Jackie's wedding, the big news in the papers was that Christian Dior had hiked up his skirt lengths to sixteen inches from the floor. The revolution of the hem line created a fashion furore, but Balenciaga was holding back and keeping dresses still close to the ankle. It was clear, in all the fashion columns, that Dior was expected to win. Dior was also using slim skirts.

Jackie, I reflected, had him beat. She had already been slimming her skirts and wearing them shorter.

I heard that the year after she was married, Jackie went back to college—Georgetown University, this time—to study political history to be able to participate more intelligently in her husband's political world. She also studied more languages—Italian, for one. I loved the stories I heard from her classmates and friends about her. One was that a student commented to her that her name sounded a lot like that of the Senator. "That's strange," he said. "Yes," she said, "isn't it?" And she hadn't mentioned that she was the Senator's wife.

I would hear stories of how she was dressing the part of the college girl, just as she had dressed the part of the girl reporter. She was wearing flat shoes and skirts and sweaters.

But a true Jacqueline touch, which I relished, was that sometimes she would take her dog along to school and would also bring her maid to hold the dog on its leash some distance from the building, and wait for the end of her class, since she couldn't take it into the classroom. Then, class over, dog and maid and mistress would all march the four or five blocks back home. Jackie told a friend she didn't want her dog to be lonely and that's why she took it along. Mary had a little lamb, but Jackie had a pooch.

When I heard the way Jackie was living, with a household staff of cook and butler and time for many trips, I remembered a column she had done in which she had asked, "Do the rich enjoy life more than the poor?" One fellow, a salesman, had answered, "I think there's something wrong with them if they don't."

Jackie really did seem to be enjoying life and she had adjusted a bit to the Senator's casual way of living by becoming a more casual dresser herself, walking around Georgetown, with her husband or alone, in slacks and shirt or sweater. Once, from my taxi window on a visit back home, I saw them both thus attired, but I didn't tell the driver to stop and I only waved.

Meanwhile my own life in Baltimore seemed to go very well. The girls were adjusted to the new surroundings and the new schools and were, in fact, fighting over the same boyfriend. I had changed jobs, after learning enough about mass production of dresses to see it was not for me after all. But I was still designing dresses on the side. My new employer was a high fashion women's specialty store which is very popular in Baltimore.

I had started in the alteration and fitting department, but suddenly I was promoted to be assistant to the manager. I couldn't figure out this sudden advancement and it wasn't until about four years later, at a farewell luncheon the store gave me when I was returning to Washington, that I found out why this had happened.

One day the manager had asked me who some of my old customers had been and I mentioned Mrs. Styles Bridges and Mrs. B. B. Hickenlooper and Mrs. Julius Wadsworth and many others, including Mrs. Walter Lippmann, Mrs. John L. Strauss, Mrs. Arthur Krock, Mrs. John F. Kennedy and Mrs. Hugh D. Auchincloss.

The store, unknown to me, had sent them each a letter, saying that I had performed duties "in a manner which leads us to believe that she has executive ability." The letter then asked, "Would you, in the strictest confidence, give us any information you have, or any opinion you may have formed, as to her ability or character, or any other information you may desire to give, so that we might be in a better position to decide as to her future with our firm?"

It was the wonderful letters that the store had received and saved—and eventually presented to me—that had resulted in my getting such a sudden advancement to a splendid position. I was especially grateful when I read Jacqueline's letter in which she said that both her mother and she thought the world of me, "not only as a dressmaker but as a person," and that she hoped they would "see fit to give Mrs. Rhea a higher position."

It was in the summer of 1955 that the poor health I had mentioned to Jacqueline two years before erupted into a raging pain and I keeled over in the store. I was rushed to the hospital and operated on immediately for a ruptured cyst. The girls were sent to Lafayette, Louisiana, to stay with an aunt and because of my health, on my doctor's advice, I let them stay there for the rest of the school year.

Christmas, 1955, looked pretty bleak. Doctor's bills and

supporting two schoolgirls a long distance away kept me
from getting ahead enough to take a trip to see the girls
over the holiday. It would be the first Christmas we had
not been together. And, to make the situation even
bleaker, the girls had recently lost their father. He had
stepped out of his car, suffered a heart attack and fallen
dead.

As the holiday approached I thought of how happy the
old days in Washington had been when the girls and I
were together and life had been one big open house with
happy sounds and cheerful customers coming in. I remembered the Christmas of 1952 when my girls had laughed
uproariously at a story Jackie had written about gift
wrapping. For it she had sketched some department store
clerks trying to gift wrap a piano.

I was certainly lonely for the old life and suddenly I felt
I would even have been happy to see the customers flick
their ashes all over my piano and park their cigarettes
on it.

But my homesickness for Washington and the old days
was forgotten when the owner of the store, Mr. Samuel J.
Schleisner, arranged for me to take a trip to Louisiana to
be with Jimi and Sylvia. Not only did I see Sylvia and
Jimi, but I got to see almost all my brothers and sisters for
the first time in many years. I even saw Chryssie who had
gone with the girls because Sylvia could not part with her.
She still looked no bigger than a small-sized white muff.

As soon as possible Jimi came back to Baltimore, but
Sylvia decided to stay in Louisiana and go to Southwestern
Louisiana Institute. Jimi graduated from high school in
Baltimore and was first to get married. I thought of how
Lee Bouvier, too, had beaten her older sister to the altar
and decided not to get upset about it or try to keep Jimi
single a while longer. It's good I didn't try to hold her back

because Sylvia did not marry till 1960, when I had once again returned to Washington and once again left it.

Much had happened by then, to be sure. For one thing, I had remarried in August, 1957. The children were so busy with their own lives they no longer were dependent on me. And my husband, who was a construction engineer, listened to my pleas to go back to Washington, where I still felt I belonged.

In January, 1958, back I came to Washington, bag, baggage and mirror. By now another Maltese dog—Snow Flurry—had taken Chryssie's place with me, and it was almost as if I had never been away. I had sent announcements in advance, and almost before I had the plaque, "Mini Rhea, Custom Dressmaker" up on a house, where I had lived before, my old customers were back. How happy I was to see them! Mrs. Curtis Munson was the first. Then came Mrs. Krock and Mrs. Sparkman and Mrs. Husted and Mrs. Harriman.

I had kept track of Jackie's life and experiences: the move to a country home in Virginia, Jack's operation on his back not long after they were married—he'd been on crutches awhile. Jackie's breaking her ankle playing touch football at Hyannis Port. Jackie learning to water ski. Jackie trying to cut down on cigarettes.

One of my customers showed me a riotous dissertation written by a friend of theirs on how to prepare for a visit with the whole Kennedy clan at Hyannis Port and how to behave while there.

It warned the prospective guests not to come at all if they didn't want to play football. But if they did come, it urged them to bone up on all political reading matter, not omitting the *Congressional Record, The Democratic Digest* and *U.S. News and World Report.*

Then on the football "field" the instructions were simply to "show raw guts and make a lot of noise."

"To show raw guts," the instructions continued, "fall on your face now and then, smash into the house once in a while . . . and laugh off a twisted ankle."

I'd enjoyed hearing about the Inaugural party she had attended in 1957—four years after the Inaugural Day she had shared with the world in her *Times-Herald* articles. This 1957 party, attended by losing Democrats, had been called an "Anti-Inaugural Ball." It had been given in Georgetown by Mr. and Mrs. Samuel Jackson Lanahan. And what had intrigued me was that the hostess, called "Scottie" by everyone, was the daughter of the American author, F. Scott Fitzgerald.

Jackie had experienced sorrow and great joy. She had known the pain of losing a child before its birth. Her beloved father, Jack Bouvier, had died in 1957. But Jackie had also known the thrill of motherhood, and after baby Caroline was born, in November of 1957, she and the Senator had moved back from Virginia to 3307 N Street, N.W., in Georgetown.

Jacqueline's sister's life had not been standing still either. Lee's marriage to Michael Canfield had not worked out and she had divorced him and married again. Now she was a Princess, wife of the Polish nobleman, Prince Stanislas Radziwill.

And what an unusual prince! He could have been a Kennedy, so well did he enter into the spirit of the campaign after the Senator captured the Democratic Presidential nomination in 1960. Radziwill came from London, where he and Lee lived, and toured the country, campaigning among the Polish-speaking groups, winning votes for his brother-in-law.

Mrs. Auchincloss was a surprise campaigner, too. Although a Republican, she nevertheless gave Democratic fund-raising teas at Merrywood. She even enlisted the aid

of her irresistible French poodle—"Charles of the Ritz"—
who shook paws to win votes.

And my life hadn't stood still either. I guess no life does.
My marriage was not a success. I went to Philadelphia because it had a reputation for culture and was not too far
from the Washington I still loved. This time I started as a
secretary in a retail store—Gimbel's, to be exact.

Then fate spun the wheel of fortune for me again and
when the wheel stopped, what was at the point of the arrow
but a tiny little Maltese that looked so much like Snow
Flurry I stopped to talk to it! How did I know this dog
would bring me good fortune?

The Maltese turned out to have the name of Horace
and at the other end of the leash there was attached a
kindly man who talked awhile about Horace and then
asked me what work I did.

I must have sounded very wistful. "I'm supposed to be
a dress designer. I really *am* a dress designer, but I've been
working as a secretary since I've been in Philadelphia."

Before I knew it, he was arranging for me to meet his
wife to discuss dress designing. I did some work for her.
She was a lovely woman—another Mrs. Auchincloss—and
within a month she had helped me find a lovely location
at 2016 Walnut Street, just off Rittenhouse Square, and had
helped me open a new shop. I didn't need that old bronze
plaque. Now I had a signmaker paint right on the display
window that wonderful word, "Designer." In fact, the
whole legend said:

DESIGNER   MINI RHEA   DRESSMAKER

Through the wording of my name was painted a
threaded needle.

I felt on top of the world. Now I could go full steam

ahead. Now I would create gowns and have the career of
which I had dreamed so long. And little by little, one customer told another about me and soon I had such wonderful customers as Countess Valdé, and a talented assistant—
Henri Di Mezzes, whom I called Hank.

Now I could relax and enjoy the political hoopla, excitement and pageantry. It was almost as if Jackie was back
at the *Times-Herald*. True, she wasn't interviewing people,
but she was writing a little campaign column of sidelights
on the campaign from her own intimate standpoint. Again
I was experiencing adventure through her eyes—rushing
to planes, taping a show with Henry Fonda in a three-way
hookup (Fonda in New York, Jack in California and she
in Washington); waiting for the Senator's daily phone calls
and trying to explain to Caroline why Daddy was being
presented with an Indian war bonnet.

I hauled out one of her old feature stories, dated November 19, 1952, which captured the excitement in Washington of the change of the political reins from one party to
the other. This was the moment when the victorious General Eisenhower came to visit President Truman after
the election.

The headline was: THRONGS 4 DEEP AT WHITE
HOUSE AS IKE APPEARS.

The sketches with which Jackie illustrated her hilarious
story were utterly delightful. First Jackie quoted the conversation she overheard between a frustrated father and
his stubborn little daughter.

" 'Saundrea,' said her father, 'who's coming by in a few
minutes?'

" 'President Truman,' came the answer.

" 'Saundrea,' said her father, 'you know better than that.
Who're you out here to watch?'

" 'President Truman,' she replied."

Then Jackie talked with a little boy named Warren

who was watching for Ike's motorcade from the top of a concrete post. He was covered with "44 Eisenhower buttons, 6 stickers and a 'Vet-for-Eisenhower' hat."

Jackie asked him about his getup as she sketched him and he scoffed, "This is nothing. Mom wouldn't let me wear my other hundred buttons."

She also sketched three sailors who were killing time photographing the famous Lafayette Park squirrels across the street from the White House as they waited and one of them, suddenly realizing their chief mission, said, "I hope to Pete he gets here before I use up all my pictures on the squirrels."

The only disgruntled voice in the crowd was that of a pitchman who had come from Baltimore to sell Eisenhower buttons and pennants. He complained to Jacqueline, "Hey, what's the matter with this town? They told me over in Baltimore you was all Republicans here. That's why I came over. And I didn't sell hardly a button. A lot of undercover Democrats, that's what I think you've got here."

Jackie's 1960 campaign column now, in the last days before the election, had a more solemn air than her old *Times-Herald* column.

She now told about the "listening parties" at her home during the televised Nixon-Kennedy debates and wrote that, among the women she had talked to, "without exception the issue uppermost in every woman's mind is peace —not a single person put the budget first. Next came education, medical care for the aged and the cost of living."

She wrote how she had felt a lump in her throat when she heard her husband comment in a debate, "I do not want future historians to say 'these were the years when the tide ran out for America'; I want them to say 'these were the years when the tide came in and America started to move again.'"

She proudly quoted Kennedy as saying, "One woman is worth ten men" when it comes to campaigning.

And she told about life in Hyannis Port, where she was waiting for the birth of her second child. And how, when a hurricane knocked down ten trees and blew part of their roof away, Caroline had not been worried for herself as much as she had been for Mitten, the kitten, Charley, the puppy and Jack, the Daddy. Everybody was found to be safe, including her Daddy who was campaigning in Texas at the time.

I wrote Jacqueline a letter and told her of my good fortune.

For the first time the letter I received was typed and had been dictated to someone, but the signature was her own.

That was the first time Jacqueline had addressed me by my first name. How I wished she could visit me now. How I wanted to discuss fashion with her and leaf through French fashion magazines again and thank her for the help she had been. I longed to reminisce about how our paths had diverged. I had gone further into the fashion world and she had followed her husband into politics.

I thought about Robert Frost's poem which painted the picture so much better than I could. "Two roads diverged in a yellow wood . . ."* in which Frost wonders what would have happened had he taken the other road in life.

I wondered, as I watched the campaign progress, if Jacqueline remembered that when she covered the 1953 Inaugural she had interviewed someone who had talked excitedly about Robert Frost, the great New Hampshire poet. She had taken the picture of one of the float builders and had asked him who had been his greatest teacher.

He had told her about studying under Robert Frost— whom he called "one of the greatest living men"—when he

* *The Road Not Taken,* Robert Frost.

Mrs. John F. Kennedy
3307 N Street N.W.
Washington 7, D.C.

Miss Mini Rhea
2016 Walnut Street
Philadelphia 3, Penna.

November 4, 1960

Dear Mini,

I'm so sorry not to have answered
your letter sooner. As you know,
I did not accompany my husband to
Philadelphia, so was not able to
get in touch with you.

The dress designing shop sounds
fine and I wish you every success.

Sincerely yours,

Mrs. John F. Kennedy

3307 N Street N.W.
Washington 7, D.C.

was in prep school. He told how Frost had maintained a close relationship with his pupils and had called it an experience he would never forget. I had learned something from Jackie's column that day which I hadn't known: Frost had won the Pulitzer prize three times.

I had told her how I loved Frost's work and she'd said, "So do I. He's t-rrific. Great and inspiring."

Again, in 1961, I wondered if Jackie remembered her column when her husband was being inaugurated as President of the United States. During this impressive ceremony I could hardly believe my eyes. There on the platform was a poet—the first poet ever to participate in this great political event—and he read a poem.

Old now, and white-haired and a little feeble he was, and a little shaken by the wind and the cold and the glare of the sun in his eyes.

But great he was, too, as he threw away his script and spoke from memory. My heart thrilled as I heard the voice of Robert Frost.

CHAPTER 16

SHE'S NOTED, SHE'S QUOTED—
SHE'S PROMOTED!

No ONE rejoiced more than I that Jackie was now our First Lady. Yet it was a Hollywood finish that sounded too good to be true. With all the strikes against her and the Senator, I had hardly dared hope till the election returns sounded the victory signal. There had been such a bombardment of brickbats, so many points of attack—Jack's low attendance record in the Senate, his religion, his youth, his wealth, his father's wealth, his father's political record, his family's helping hand in the campaign and the perfectly ridiculous charge that, since one of his sisters was married to a Hollywood star who was a friend of Frank Sinatra—Peter Lawford—Sinatra would be butting into affairs at the White House.

There had been the complaint that Jacqueline hadn't travelled with her husband throughout the campaign as Mrs. Nixon had.

Even Jackie's clothes, hairdo and her very look were coming under fire. Unflattering words like "floor mop hairdo" appeared in the press. But the old Jackie I knew came charging in to her own defense. In her campaign letter she wrote, "All the talk over what I wear and how I fix my hair has me amused and puzzles me. What does my hairdo have to do with my husband's ability to be President?"

I loved that answer. Then, just before election, there were the eleventh hour attacks on Jacqueline's clothes budget. She was accused of spending $30,000 a year abroad on her wardrobe. Her answer was typically "Jackie" and could have come right out of one of her old *Times-Herald* columns: "I couldn't spend that much unless I wore sable underwear."

I laughed till I cried. It was just as if I were back in the fitting room in Georgetown, reading her *Times-Herald* column. I thought, ruefully, I hope her sense of humor doesn't scare off votes for her husband. Because now, instead of the interviewer, she was the important one, the one interviewed, and the nation hung on every word she uttered.

I thought of the old two-liner I had made up about her when she was going to "visit the Queen" and made up a variation:

> She's noted,
> She's quoted.

The rest of her defense of her clothes-buying habits should have been reassuring to women who feared she might set an example of extravagance or might be so oriented to France that she would be shunning things labelled American. In answer to these "suppositions," Jackie said that she never bought more than one suit or coat in a season from Balenciaga or Givenchy and that she bought many dresses off department store racks for $29 or

$39, and also that some of her clothes she had had made by "a little dressmaker in Washington."

Yes, that was certainly true. Jackie would indeed buy dresses off the racks and then let me, her little dressmaker, give them the couturier look. I remember that sometimes several at a time would come to me directly from the New York and Washington stores.

I would take out my muslin pattern of her exact figure and go ahead with the alterations, letting out a bit here, taking in a bit there, shortening, if necessary and, of course, adding my "magic dart" to improve the bustline.

The result had been a look of elegance far exceeding what the original cost of the gown would indicate. I hoped that women all over the country would realize how Jackie managed to look so well in inexpensive dresses and would do likewise.

After the election I breathed a sigh of relief and again revised my "poem." Now it was even better than going to visit the Queen. She now would entertain and be entertained by kings and queens. I jotted down a four line version:

> She's noted,
> She's quoted,
> And now, to the top,
> She's promoted.

But the humor went out of the situation one day soon after the election, when the phone in my Philadelphia shop rang and it was a reporter from *Women's Wear Daily* —Trudy Prokop. "Are you the Mini Rhea who used to be a dressmaker for Mrs. Kennedy?" she asked.

"Oh, no, how did you find me?" I groaned.

Publicity that would take advantage of Jacqueline's new position was the last thing I wanted. And in my new shop in Philadelphia I never volunteered the information that

I had sewn for the wife of the President, or even mentioned I knew her, unless someone asked me.

"Can I come to see you? We would like to do a story on Jacqueline Kennedy's taste in clothes."

I could hardly deny that I had sewn for Jackie Bouvier in the old days and, with my own experience as a former newspaper woman, I realized Miss Prokop had a job to do.

The *Women's Wear Daily* carried the first story about me under Trudy Prokop's by-line, entitled, "Philadelphia New Locale for Jackie's 'Little Dressmaker.'"

After this story appeared, my phone hardly left me time to sew—or to do anything else, for that matter.

One of the funniest situations developed from a phone call I received the night I dashed home in a hurry to dress for a fashion group meeting. I was just ready for the tub when the ring came and, thinking it was my assistant calling to remind me of something, I hurriedly picked up the phone. When I heard the operator say, "I have Miss Rhea on the line," I wondered, what on earth? Then I heard a man say, "This is CBS News calling." I almost dropped the receiver and all I could think of was my bath water running merrily. So if that reporter reads this and if he thought at the time that I was a little curt in my answers, maybe he will now understand why. The water *did* run over.

Newspaper after newspaper called, wanting to know all about Mrs. Kennedy's likes and dislikes in fashion, and what her favorite colors were.

Part of the time I'd be all tense and reluctant about telling anything, and Kittie Campbell, in her story in the Philadelphia *Bulletin,* said that interviewing me was about as hard as trying to squeeze secrets out of the FBI Chief, J. Edgar Hoover.

Then I'd find my reporter's instinct taking over and I'd reveal that Jackie had liked "a pink, a very strong pink, a hot pink, and also white," and that I had made many dresses with French influence for her, and sometimes had even copied a dress or suit from a picture in the French fashion magazines. Suddenly pink and hot pink were big news.

But dates were always hard for me to remember and, catching me off guard that way, I made several boo-boos on what year this or that had happened.

From the *New York World Telegram and Sun* to the *San Francisco Examiner,* clippings of whole columns were being sent to me by friends. But, of course, since I was now in Philadelphia, what thrilled me most was to pick up the local papers and see an interview with a picture of myself. Even Snow Flurry made the papers and was reported as "screening everyone thoroughly" as they came into my establishment though I didn't dare hurt his feelings by telling him that one paper had erroneously called him a "toy white poodle" instead of a rare Maltese.

Peggy Bauer of the *Philadelphia Daily News* used a photograph of me at my drawing board for her story and quoted my comment about the First Lady-elect: "I knew *her* when and she knew *me* when." She told how I summed up Jacqueline's taste with one word, "simplicity," and how I had reported that Jackie didn't like a cluttered look or too much jewelry, and that she loved beautiful fabrics.

Others reported my prediction that Jackie would do for the American women's fashions what the Prince of Wales had done for British men's tailoring in the Twenties.

It was really a strange and, I must admit, thrilling feeling to see my Washington career spread out in the newspapers from coast to coast—how I had come to Philadelphia to establish myself as a "dress designer" rather than a "little dressmaker."

And even how dresses of my design had been worn by famous guests at every Inaugural Ball since 1948. And

204 / I Was Jacqueline Kennedy's Dressmaker

how I had made the gowns for a whole wedding party for a friend of Mrs. Eisenhower, who had attended the wedding when she was our First Lady.

Yes, those were certainly exciting days—those days in November, 1960, right after the election, when I was quoted as saying, "To me she was just a lovely young girl. I never dreamed that she would be famous" and "She has an elegant figure and anything she wears immediately becomes chic and smart. She's a fashion designer's delight."

I submitted my design for the Inaugural Ball gown through *Women's Wear* which also collected those of several other designers.

A few reporters commented in stories that I was the "sentimental favorite."

As it turned out, Jacqueline Kennedy did what she loved to do most—she designed her own Inaugural gown. But I was thrilled to see how close our thinking still was. Anyone who wishes to can check statements in the newspapers of the time. *Women's Wear,* for example, reported on November 14 that I would like to see Mrs. Kennedy wear "a sheath, preferably white, in a heavily beaded crepe or chiffon." All the other papers also reported that I had chosen for her the ultra-slim look and beading on "heavy crepe or chiffon."

The actual gown I designed, a sketch of which is included in this book, was a sheath of white chiffon over crepe, with a straight panel hanging as a train from the shoulders to the floor, to create a very regal effect. The neckline I chose was just a little lower than the one she designed for herself, with an irregular edging at the neck. In my version the beading on the chiffon covered the whole gown. In Mrs. Kennedy's version, the beading was under the chiffon and came only to the waist, the embroidery being screened by the chiffon overblouse.

At the Inaugural Ball her pencil slim white
sheath with chiffon overblouse stood out
dramatically in the sea of bouffant dresses.
She designed it herself ... Overblouses were in!

When the President saw his First Lady come down the staircase their first night in the White House, as they were leaving for the Ball, he said the words that every woman cherishes. "My dear, I have never seen you look lovelier."

He looked pretty good himself in white tie and tails, with his hair not tousled now, but neat and cropped and looking somehow tamed. In fact, so good did he look these days that two months after he was in office he was included in the list of the nation's "Ten Best Dressed Men."

I couldn't have been more amused, remembering the non-sartorial path which he'd travelled to reach this eminence. The Fashion Foundation of America, which selected him, admitted, tongue in cheek, that in the past Kennedy had been a "controversial fashion figure," but that his new "get-down-to-business appearance" was being copied by many other men.

Jackie had made the list of "Best Dressed Women" just before the Inauguration, and I like to think she deserved it for her independence and individuality.

I had watched with great interest Jackie's growth and development in fashioning her own look back in the early Fifties, but I had not dreamed that some day "her look" would become almost every woman's look. I had expected her to make American styles more popular, but I did not anticipate she would become such an outstanding fashion leader that whole clothing industries would take their cue from her. Nor that I, too, would be copying her styles—just as in the old days.

I had first seen her wear the back-of-the-head pillbox in 1954 when her husband went to the hospital for the operation on his back. But in 1961, when she wore that type of hat to her husband's Inauguration and to every daytime affair thereafter, with many small variations in style and color, the pillbox became a multimillion dollar business and some stores reported that up to seventy per cent of their hat business was in pillboxes. I made some pillboxes myself for customers to match their dresses or suits.

And then, when everyone was "bubble top" oriented, Jacqueline came back from Paris in a darling hat—a cloche that could have come right out of the flapper era of the flaming Twenties—and caused another flip-flop among my customers.

She wore an overblouse at the Inaugural Ball and suddenly half of my customers were ordering overblouses to make their pre-Inaugural dresses look like Jackie's.

She carried a muff at the Inauguration and wore a cloth coat. Of course muffs were immediately "in" and full fur coats were briefly "out." Customers started bringing me little collar and muff sets, asking me to make a coat to go with them.

Jacqueline liked a standing cuff suit collar that formed a frame around her face. Instantly, even women with short necks were demanding that I make the same for them.

Her sleeveless, collarless, unornamented sheath dress was labelled the "Jackie look" and became a uniform to a nation of women, whether their arms could take the exposure or not. Thank goodness, I thought, at least most women look better without collars, or the men would start leaving the country.

Jackie wore a Grecian dress to her first state dinner in the White House, honoring President and Mrs. Habib Bourguiba of Tunisia and, before I could pronounce "Bourguiba," even bathing suits sported a Grecian drape, with one shoulder exposed.

One evening gown she wore on her first visit to foreign soil as First Lady—Canada—had slits in the skirt almost to the knee. Suddenly that was fashion right, fashion bright, thanks to the Chinese.

Other than that, the evening dresses she preferred were simple sheaths made of exquisite materials, some quite ornate, and therefore hardly a customer would now put on a strapless evening gown. Everyone wanted the prim, covered-up look, the unbroken-front look.

I was very amused when one fashionable Philadelphian came to me and said, "I want the ultimate in the Jackie look. Just take two straight pieces of cloth and sew them together at the shoulder and sides, leaving room for my head and arms to get through. Ignore the waistline. Make it tight at the sides, but leave slits in the side seams just below the knees, down to the floor."

I started to laugh. "Don't laugh," she said. "It's funny, I know, but I mean it. That's the gown I want you to make."

And darned if it didn't look pretty good when it was made up in exotic Chinese brocade. Straight and slim, with a straight-across, bateau neckline and a Chinese slit skirt. I think if Jackie had seen it, she would have said, "T-rrific," or used the new word which I hear has become her current favorite, "Fantastic."

Jackie has, through her example, made women look more chic. And her straight simplicity has been called by some style experts the "Continental look," because her styles are definitely in the European tradition.

But the major point I would like to make is that all of the fashions which Jackie has favored have suddenly become high fashion—the open-necked look, even on suits, the loose waists, the boxy jackets, the dresses with unbroken lines, the overblouse. All these preferences are those which Jackie had long before she was in the White House. And she had also liked braid edging on suits and dresses long before that. And, of course, shocking pink, bright pink, hot pink—or call it what you will.

Many of these trends I saw her developing years ago. It isn't that Jacqueline Kennedy has changed. It is that the nation has caught up with her. This illustrates that Jacqueline Kennedy believes in wearing exactly what is right for her.

She has kept evolving and improving her special styles. And so well do they look on her that now women and girls all over the country dream of looking as well in them as she does.

Many of these ideas, such as overblouses for sports, came to her in the early Fifties and I executed them for her. Jackie has not invented entirely new styles for herself, but has modified or elaborated them for more important occasions.

The dresses Jackie wore in 1952 were almost identical to what she is now wearing for daytime. Before, they were playtime dresses; now they are daytime dresses.

Colorful cotton prints, light-weight cottons, some Liberty cottons and some plain colored fabrics were what she liked. These were made with a semi-low round neckline, sleeveless, with a fitted bodice and full, gathered skirts— not gored. The dresses she's wearing today are very similar, only the waistlines are a little more relaxed and the skirts are not quite as full, some of them having box pleats.

I can't remember her ever wearing a very low neck— except for her evening gowns which were strapless. The neckline always came just a little below or above the collarbone. She liked a wide, sleeveless look, rather than a narrow strap over the shoulders.

The greatest change in the look of Jacqueline's clothes through the years has been in the de-emphasis of her bustline and waistline. When she developed her almost straight-up-and-down look, shoulder to hemline, she did a great service to more than half the American women who were caught up in the national adulation of the Marilyn Monroe and Gina Lollobrigida figures, full-busted, small-waisted, round-hipped.

Now those who are not built like these two movie stars

can come into their own and stop padding their figures. They have the greatest champion possible to help them take courage in emphasizing the youthful, boyish, slim look. For this I say three cheers for Jacqueline. She has succeeded in doing what fashion experts have been unable to do for two generations—popularize the small-busted, slim-looking figure.

When Jacqueline announced that she had appointed Oleg Cassini as her official designer, many people wondered if her styles would change drastically to conform to his views, but I was sure that Jackie would remain Jackie and would keep to her own style.

Cassini had become famous for dresses as tight as a second skin—a style Jackie had matured beyond, growing into the more elegantly relaxed look.

The designer had been the talk of the fashion world for the amusing and scandalous names he gave his creations, such as "Navel Operation" for a bare-midriff style and "Missionary's Downfall" for a gown with a most revealing neckline. Cassini himself had said, "Maybe if Mrs. Kennedy had heard some of the names, she wouldn't have picked me." But I must say that he did a wonderful job in adjusting to her style and has designed some of the most lovely and elegant dresses I have ever seen, utilizing the same straight, relaxed lines and understated look she had worked out for herself.

And I have noticed that some of his designs were modified from his original sketch in the making of the finished garment. One ball gown of pink ribbed silk organza, designed to have three tiers of ruffles rising to a point in front, was simplified, by the time Jackie wore it in Ottawa, to have the ruffles in three straight lines across the bottom of the skirt.

One change Cassini may have wrought is in possibly introducing a new color in Jacqueline's wardrobe. He designed one bright green dress for her. I saw pictures of it in a fashion magazine, but I have never read of her wearing it. When I knew her, I don't recall working on a single green dress.

I am sure that the reason she chose to work with only one couturier was to halt the avalanche of designs which must have poured in on her from every direction—including mine. Besides, Cassini, who studied art abroad, has the Continental touch she likes, but still strikes a genuine American note.

I was interested to learn that Oleg's mother, Countess Cassini, was also a fashion designer in Italy after the family was stranded there when the Russian Revolution barred them from their homeland.

I am sure that another reason Jacqueline Kennedy chose one designer to look after her needs and co-ordinate her wardrobe accessories was that she wanted to be free to give fuller attention to the raising of Caroline and her new son, John Fitzgerald, Jr., and the tremendous job she had undertaken, that of refurnishing the White House with authentic antiques of the proper historic period.

When the announcement of the birth of a son came, I thought of the little jingle she had used in her column on superstitions:

> One crow, sorrow
> Two crows, joy
> Three crows, a wedding
> Four crows, a boy.

The First Lady is deeply concerned and striving for greater privacy and protection for her children. She has put a halt to so much picture-taking of Caroline and ordered a screen of bushes to shield the little girl at play. I remember when, in 1952, she asked people if they would like their sons to grow up to be President and one man said, "No, that's not a human life, being constantly with a bodyguard."

But in spite of the constraint of the White House, with the confinement of its constant security watch, and the grave duties of entertainment and diplomacy, Jackie, I am happy to hear, has become more like her mother in enjoying, as she does, every little fun detail about the children.

Mother and daughter have many a laugh over Caroline. For example, when Caroline insisted on buying her own present for her baby brother and picked a comb for his non-existent hair.

And Jackie laughs over her own gags, for she is still a practical joker. One day she showed Jack an abstract painting for which she claimed she had paid some outrageous price. Only after she had stunned the President completely, did she let him in on the fact that the painter had been none other than that gifted American primitive, Caroline, age three. Jackie gets her laughs too from her husband's quick humor which sparkles best in the tight spots. For example, when he was presenting a medal to America's first astronaut, Commander Shepard, and first forgot to pin it on the man, then dropped it when he finally started to pin it on, he said sheepishly, "You're getting this from the ground up."

Together, Jack and Jackie enjoyed the outrageous signs French students carried in Paris to show Jackie how they felt about her: "Jacqui go home—my home!" And they listed their addresses and telephone numbers.

But for every moment of fun, there are the worrisome moments and the tiresome moments when the show must go on. And worst of all, there are the attacks on her personal taste in clothes. No matter how hard she may try to please, no First Lady seems to have escaped the wagging tongues and the criticism in the press. Jackie has not escaped it either.

There have been complaints that Jackie wore her skirts too short and her hair too long. That she once went bare-legged to church on a high holy day, Good Friday. That pillbox hats are not dignified enough . . .

That having only one dress designer isn't fair to other dress designers. That she should buy some dresses overseas to show good will. That she should *not* buy dresses over-seas to show she is an American all the way. That she *did* buy some clothes from Paris *sub rosa*. That Cassini's gowns are copied from the French. That one gown Cassini made for her Paris trip was so like one the wife of a top French official had ordered from Pierre Cardin's spring collection that Jackie didn't dare wear it in Paris. That another gown Cassini made for the First Lady was practically identical with the one he had whipped up for his sister-in-law, Mrs. Igor Cassini, who wore hers one day before Jacqueline did . . .

That her dresses look too much alike. That they are too uncomplicated and simple. That they are not simple enough. That she should never wear bare arms in daytime. That she should wear more fur to help the fur industry. That she should wear more wool to help the wool industry, and ditto for the cotton industry.

I could go on, for the complaints are endless. But so is the praise she is getting from other quarters. I belong in the cheering section. I would like to go on record here as defending all her decisions because she is a remarkable individual and has the right to her own convictions. She is our First Lady, but she is still Jacqueline Kennedy, in-comparable individualist. And I would like to make an even bet that she will not change radically until she has arrived at a change through gradual evolution. She will not be dictated to.

Knowing how she feels about hats, I'm sure that she chose the pillbox because it interferes least with the design of a dress and, in the front view, offers merely a line of color in a halo effect across the top of the hair. It does not cut height. It does not detract from the face.

I was happy to hear that not long ago, when Jackie was flying back to Washington, she had with her a sketch pad such as I was used to seeing. She was sketching some dress designs, just as I had watched her do. My only regret is that I couldn't be there to see the sketches—and her.

But life goes in circles. Who knows. . . ?

A Sketchbook
of
Jackie's fashion history

One of the first ball gowns I made for Jackie in
the winter of '51 — pink peau de soie with silver
braid in geometric pattern. Eventually the
braid started to dance before my eyes

Jackie always had several black
suits in her wardrobe. Toward the
end of our association they were
starting to be less pinched in at the
waist and the collar stood a little
away from the neck . . .

I admired her modesty in the sport togs she ordered

white
I made a halter swim suit
and matching jacket for poolside,
with bright orangy print lining

She never overdressed for work. This blue
step-in dress, which she designed, had black
braid edging on white collar and cuffs

Christmas, 1952 — Jackie in a red velvet
floor-length stole on a white satin gown — a
lovely holiday look. Jackie designed all her
own evening gowns. The Senator approved!

Courtesy American Weekly

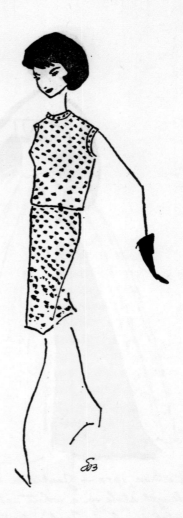

She liked polka dots...

... and she still likes
polka dots — even for evening

*The most elegant things are the most
utterly simple. Jackie often let her lovely
materials form their own and only ornamentation*

*I frequently used braid
edging for Jackie's dresses
and suits.*

Foreign students, visiting on the White House lawn, found Jackie still likes braid trim for suits and dresses, just as when <u>she</u> was a student, a (in 1954) career girl and once again a student

The start of the "Jackie look"

When I knew her the Jackie type dress
was her playtime dress, snug-waisted
and with gathered skirt . . .

... but today it has evolved into her daytime dress, with slimmer skirt and relaxed waistline. Often her pearls are tucked inside the neckline

Before the White House she wore this one in a pale yellow check with a short overblouse...

. . . but in the White House she prefers the longer overblouse. Here it is in straw-colored ottoman silk, worn with pearls at a White House luncheon for the press

One sleeveless, collarless dress, made in the
spring of '53, could fit into her wardrobe today as
far as style goes. But it had a pink flowered design...

*... and today she prefers
solid colors ...*

It has also
become her
"after five" look

. . . or self color design which is woven
into the material, as in this brocade

Jackie avoided square necklines, and used a slanting or irregular line in her hairdo or dress to minimize the effect of her square-shaped face

Here the off-center effect is nicely achieved by a sweep of ruffle from shoulder to hem

Jackie liked the off-center effect, but this particular button arrangement made Jackie's wide-set eyes look still farther apart and the line across the skirt cut her height

When I was her "little dressmaker" she always wore strapless gowns for evening . . .

. . . and still continued to wear them after she was married. But eventually they became slim and relaxed, like this heavy satin

... but even before her engagement to Senator
Kennedy she had started to relax the waistlines a
bit and reduce the bouffant skirt

I felt her wedding costume, which took 50 yards
of ivory tissue silk taffeta, was just not Jackie.
It lacked her usual simplicity and had
excessive ornamentation of ruffles, tucks,
stitchings, flowers, jewelry and veil. I would
have preferred to see her in the simplest of lines
so that her rosepoint veil— a family heirloom—
would be the important feature. Her wedding
gown reminded me of . . .

This was the Jackie look at the 1956 convention when the Senator almost captured the Vice-Presidential nomination — but the V-neck has not been a Jackie favorite in the White House

Jackie has always been well suited to suits. This one, with elbow length sleeves, she wore in 1959 to have her picture taken by Jacques Lowe for a story by my co-author. The story appeared in The American Weekly, May 10, 1959, and one of these pictures taken in this suit became her favorite. She sent it autographed to friends and fans from the White House. That day she did not wear a hat

Never since Empress Eugenie has a woman
been more quickly and ardently copied

When she once combined orange and hot
pink for the seashore, this wild color combination
became the teenage rage, even for dress-up

With her swan-like neck she can wear standing cuff collars . . .

. . . and also the Chinese collar effect. She has worn both in the White House — and before the White House

. . . but I'm proud to say I would also have
dressed her in a slim white sheath. This is
the Inaugural gown I designed for the First
Lady and submitted through Women's Wear
Daily. It was heavily beaded chiffon over
silk crepe and had a panel hanging as a train
from shoulder to floor for regal effect

(This is my assistant's sketch)

*A casual coat with sharply contrasting
ribbed dark-colored collar she wore when
roughing it, came to mind when . . .*

... Jackie chose the same dark-light effect for
the elegant Inaugural Day coat and dress costume
at the Capitol. This time in sable contrasting with
fawn wool cloth

*Her gowns in the White House are elegant with
a French accent and the stamp of her individuality*

*In the White House she sometimes wears both
beads and a brooch pinned on off center. Her
husband, when he was President-elect, gave her a
lovely pin in a strawberry design for Christmas, 1960*

The "Jackie look" at Easter, 1961 — long overblouse, three-quarter length sleeves, pillbox hat, bouffant hair — the look that made fashion history

It was unusual to see Jackie in buttons and bows, but this "little girl" collar and scarf effect was very feminine one day at White House tea time

The First Lady loves cocktail suits
in brocade — this blue one went
to the ballet

Some of the most elegant gowns I have
ever seen her in have been designed by Cassini,
and this one of palest yellow organza in
Grecian style is my particular favorite.
Chandelier earrings are the only jewelry

Fringe was not "on a binge," but very elegantly and tastefully controlled on the gown the First Lady wore in Canada. A Cassini design

The gowns she now wears are not always as Cassini designed them. This is how Cassini planned a pink silk organza with three tiers of ruffles...

... and here is the modified version she wore in Canada — the ruffles are in straight lines

She still likes ties of self material on
dresses and coats to give a casual air and
softness to the chin line

. . . and today Jackie especially likes to have
the collar stand away from her neck. Many of
her suits, such as this pink tweed one she wore
at a Senate Ladies' Red Cross luncheon, have box
jackets. Today many of her suits are navy blue

She also likes the collars of her coats to stand
a little away from her neck, as in this darling navy
⅞ length, low pockets coat which goes . . .

... with this perfect little navy blue sheath to make a delightful travelling costume. By Cassini, of course! Note the cap sleeves

And Jackie still likes the off-center
effect, as in this Chez Ninon blue-gray suit
she brought back from her trip to Paris
as First Lady

*My favorite Cassini coat — double-
breasted, stand-away collar and still
Jackie's favorite three-quarter sleeves*

Jackie was still true to her own fashion
personality when she chose this Givenchy
coat as a gesture of friendship to France
when she said goodbye to President and
Mme. de Gaulle and to Paris. Pink
gabardine, double-breasted, three-quarter
length sleeves. Givenchy hat in white.
Shortie gloves

At the Japanese Embassy in Washington, in
shimmering satin, still with her new French
hairdo, scooped over the ears for evening.
Jacqueline's style is always developing but
still remains the "Jackie look." Thus, the
evolution of a First Lady

To church on Sunday with a little lace
scarf over her head, Jackie is still a
woman of the people

Variations on a theme . . .
    Once she'd settled on the pillbox she
thought of many variations . . . and . . .

Accessories ⟶
Simple jewelry.
Gold brooch - or
pin worn off
center

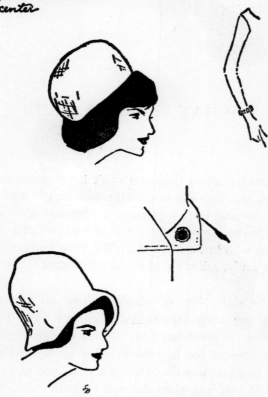

After half the American women had copied her
bubble top and pillbox hats, Jackie changed her
style for the first time by bringing back a cloche
hat from Europe . . . What next?

--✦{ CHAPTER 17 }✦--

WHAT IS ELEGANCE?

THE WOMAN doesn't live who can't be elegant. In fact, I have seen the average housewife and career and college girl transformed into a picture of elegance in one quick leap. It can be done. It should be done. *You* can do it.

Women who know I sewed for the First Lady, before she was First Lady, ask me if she looked elegant when she was a girl.

Yes, she did. Not, of course, when she was rushing around slung with camera and shoulder bag. Then, no matter how crowded her day, she always looked chic and perfectly dressed for her career. But in her quieter moments, when she was dressed for a date, she was elegance personified. Ah, yes, then she was elegant.

She was elegant because, for one thing, she walked with head held high. It is impossible to look elegant if you have bad posture, if you look meek, unsure of yourself, timid.

Elegance is assurance.

And it is much more. Elegance is a total picture, a

blending of person, personality and poise into an image of perfection.

It is a richness of effect which makes a woman the cynosure of all eyes. Now I don't mean your gown must cost five hundred dollars. It must be the best of its kind—for YOU. This involves the fit of the garment. If it has creases around the waist because it is even a bit too tight for you, you automatically lose elegance. Maybe your sister could look elegant in it, but not you.

Elegance and the too-tight look just don't go together, because that invariably gives the impression that you are trying too hard to make an impression. Elegance has a touch of the casual about it, a little of the relaxed feeling that you, yourself, are enjoying your clothes. Elegance and tenseness don't mix.

Elegance, above all, is supreme poise. How can you be poised when you look uncomfortable in a dress—and probably are? It's impossible.

Nor is there elegance in a dress that is so short you may be caught surreptitiously pulling it down.

A dress must not wobble over your body even a little as you walk, as if in search of a firm foundation. Unless you are firm as a rock and thin as a rail, you can't be elegant without a firm foundation garment. You may prefer to give society other impressions of yourself, model the pose of a Hollywood siren or a Brigitte Bardot—but you can't be wiggly and look elegant. Impossible!

Nor should an outfit be out of place. Wearing the wrong dress to the right place may make others feel uncomfortable, even if you aren't. You can become ridiculous by wearing the most elegant costume if it is out of place, such as a lovely brocade dress at a spectator sport—the bleachers, the tennis court, the poolside. Again, impossible! You must not strive for elegance at a sports affair.

And elegance is equally out of place in an office. If more girls realized this, they would, in turn, "realize" more promotions. An office is a place for efficiency. Elegance at the filing cabinet gives the impression of a poor soul loaded with fancy clothes, but devoid of judgment.

Those are some of the things that contribute to a lack of elegance.

Now let's probe further into what elegance *really* is.

Elegance is suppressed excitement, not unrestrained enthusiasm. An elegantly dressed woman may sit in a night club watching a hula dance with animation and a sparkle in her eye, but if she gets up in her beautiful evening gown and starts dancing a hula, too, she loses all the elegance the gown bestowed on her. For a hula she needs a grass skirt. "When in Rome do as the Romans do" and save the grass skirt routine for Tahiti.

Elegance is a look of knowledge and appreciation.

Elegance is, in the best sense, worldliness and sophistication.

Elegance is control. If an elegantly dressed woman has a fly-away curl, you know she knows it and likes it and has it there purposely. An elegant woman controls even her casual effects. When the press poked fun at Jackie's hairdo, calling it "mussed up," a hair stylist came to her defense. He described it as "the elegance of controlled disarray."

Elegance is not conceit, mind you, not smugness. It is simply the strength of self-possession.

On the clothes front, elegance is a sense of fitness—sport dresses for sports, gowns for galas. It is, to quote the dictionary, "propriety, expressing fastidious taste."

Elegance is underdressing rather than overdressing. Elegance is knowing when to stop. It is the look that says, "I cared enough to pay you the compliment of looking my best." It does not say, "I knocked myself out, I did everything I could think of, to impress you." That's why a woman, choked with beads at the neck, shackled with bracelets at the wrists, crowned with jewels in her hair, weighted down with pins on her dress, rings on her fingers and spangles on her shoes, cannot look elegant. She has overshot her mark. Her arrows fall to earth, she knows not where, and she wonders why she never hits the mark.

In some exotic countries, ornamentation—even over-ornamentation from our viewpoint—is extremely chic, the height of fashion. And in India, a Hindu lady, garbed in brilliant-colored saris, with many beautiful necklaces and rings, bracelets galore on arms and ankles, is supremely elegant in her surroundings. Elegance is modified by a country's customs and taste.

In the United States, elegance is always more reserved. Here an ankle chain or ankle strap is *not* elegant, nor is a superfluity of jewels.

To achieve the look of elegance you must have the feeling that you are right. This is self-possession, the noblesse oblige of the gentlemen and ladies to the manner born. Naturally, it helps greatly to be dressed right for the time and place but if, through some circumstance beyond your control, you happen not to be dressed right at the moment, poise can carry you through. Embarrassment never commands respect. Self-possession does.

A man, returning from a hunting trip, with no time to change from his grubby togs, can check into the swankiest hotel and have the bellboys hopping as though he wore imported English tweeds—if he has the *air* of being right.

This applies to women, too. A woman, playfully tricked into becoming the hostess at a "surprise" party in her honor, may have been caught in lounging pajamas, but can be the most glamorous female at the party—if she knows, and *shows* that, after all, she *was* appropriately dressed for her time and place *before* the shouts of "Surprise! Surprise!"

Elegance does not necessarily depend on fabulous fabrics or costly furs. Jacqueline Kennedy proved that when she wore a cloth coat for the Inauguration. Ah, but that was elegant. And why? Because of the chic touches—the luxurious circlet of sable around the neck and the matching fur muff she carried. Yet, had the muff and narrow collar been of dark cloth instead of expensive sable, the color contrast would have been just as effective and the ensemble just as elegant. This is true because the right design, line and color emphasis, even more than luxurious materials, are the hallmarks of elegance. And so, with taste and know-how, even a girl on a limited budget can achieve elegance.

Elegance is the *look* of luxury. And the secret of this lies in good design.

In the United States, we women are fortunate that good wholesale houses now reproduce both French and American models in less expensive adaptations. Now any woman with a moderate income can achieve a look of luxury. It doesn't take money; it takes styling, trained taste, planning and fastidiousness.

Like Cinderella's pumpkin, an elegant look can vanish instantly if gloves are soiled or a stocking seam is twisted—why not give up and use seamless hose?—and make-up is a little stale and greasy on the face. Elegance demands perfection and freshness and cleanliness, a just-stepped-out-of-a-beauty-salon-where-I-had-a-facial-and-the-works look.

Elegance is ageless. If you have added a few fine years, your chances of looking elegant are heightened. A child is not elegant. A woman must look every bit a woman and have an air of pride in her womanhood in order to attain real elegance. That is why a grown woman who tries to dress like a little girl looks anything but elegant. She may look cute, but she doesn't look elegant. Cuteness is not elegance. Maybe, in a few isolated instances, the look of cuteness, rather than elegance, is preferable for a woman. For June Allyson, who is a tiny, dainty creature, it is perfect. She is beautifully cute. There is a childlike quality to her face and figure and her little girl hairdo and *jeune fille* clothes are darling. For her. But there aren't many like her.

If you are a size ten or over, and weigh more than one hundred pounds, don't try for the little girl look. And be glad you aren't the little girl. Be glad that you are mature and can achieve an adult look of elegance. The spectacle of a child trying to look elegant by dressing up in Mummy's clothes is very amusing and makes you laugh. For a similar but opposite reason, you laugh at a big woman trying to look like a little girl in bonnet and buttons and bows, and sashes and furbelows. But this laughter has a touch of pity.

If you turn your back on cuteness and concentrate on adult glamor, there will be no pity—only admiration.

So concentrate on the grown-up, glamorous you, and you will be elegant.

Jacqueline Kennedy has given new importance to the word "elegance," because that is exactly what she has when dressed for the evening. She is as fresh as roses and gardenias, and to be near her reminds one of a sunny spring garden because of the faint touch of scent she wears.

Her make-up is always delicate and looks freshly put on. The lipstick never clashes with the dress; there is a unity, an agreement between the face and the gown. She wears her gown proudly, but naturally, and has perfect poise. She need never worry about it—it will take care of itself. She seems to feel her gown is right for her and she is pleased, yes, happy, with it. If there is anything at all worrying her, you will never see a trace of it on her face.

Her carriage is proud, her head held high. Yet it is evident that she feels the interest and warmth she conveys to people. There is never a vestige of condescension in her manner.

And her voice! Ah, how important is the voice. When Jacqueline speaks there is music in her tones. It is the King's English she speaks. No ungrammatical phrases, no sloppy enunciation. There is imagination in her choice of words. Elegance is control—even in speech. I have seen the effect of the so-called elegance which meets the eye, shattered in an instant when a supposedly elegant woman opened her mouth and released a string of coarse language, couched in bad English and shouted in a loud, coarse voice. The elegant dress could not camouflage her innate vulgarity.

But when Jacqueline Kennedy speaks her voice is low and modulated. She concentrates on the person with whom she is conversing, speaking only loud enough for him to hear. She does not sound as if she were trying to get the attention of every person in the room.

So musical is her voice that, when she was interviewed in French on television shortly before her trip to Paris with the President, and answered in fluent French the questions put to her, it was a pleasure to listen to her, even though I do not know the French language. I have been told, by some of my French customers, that Jacqueline's French is almost flawless—there is only the faintest trace of accent. I wouldn't know. I only know it is a joy to hear her charming voice.

Elegance is more than just an external trapping. Its foundation is in one's personality. It is a voice and manner that is subdued, modest, self-contained, quiet, controlled.

An elegant female may not use un-feminine language, because if she does she immediately and irrevocably loses the last shred of elegance.

So here are some definite and positive rules for a more elegant *you:*

1. Speak softly and well.
2. Stand tall and sit erectly, chin up.
3. Act assured at all times.
4. Never let a look of worry or doubt cross your face.
5. Look and be an individual. Never copy someone else's costume. Create your own touches.
6. Look sparkling clean and freshly made up—even if you have to wash your face five times a day. Some women are luckier than others in having a complexion that holds make-up longer.
7. It is safer to dress with understatement than to be overdressed.
8. Exaggerate only one detail—a dramatic swooshing stole, an out-sized scarf of brilliant hue, a striking piece of jewelry, one sharp color contrast. Or it may be an extreme hairdo, but in this case every other detail of your outfit must be underplayed.
9. Use only good materials. It is better to be dressed in the finest synthetic you can find, than in a cheap grade of sleazy silk.
10. Your dress must look absolutely unwrinkled by either folding or tightness, and it must be perfectly pressed. This means not a single wrinkle from too tight a fit *ever*.
11. Look at ease in your clothes. Without the look of comfort—or of enjoying your clothes, as Frenchwomen seem to—there is no elegance, because elegance entails ease.
12. All accessories to your dress—hat, shoes, gloves, purse, unless *one* of them is to be your eye-catching detail—must be simple.
12½. Last, but perhaps most important of all, remember that time, place and garb must form a perfect trio, or elegance is lost.

CHAPTER 18

WHAT TO WEAR AND WHEN TO WEAR IT

THE RULES for the game of looking right are actually simple—very simple. Yet how few women know them.

A sister of President Kennedy's, who helped him meet the public in his various campaigns, told friends that it had surprised her that women would wear cocktail dresses at lunchtime or in mid-afternoon.

This has disturbed me ever since because I realize these women were trying to put their best foot forward and in doing so had made a fashion *faux pas*. As someone who had to learn the hard way which garb is appropriate, I cringe for the woman who wants to do the right thing and does the wrong thing because she simply doesn't *know*.

But unfortunately the arbiters of social conduct, just as the bar of legal justice, make no allowance for ignorance.

It is a pity that we do not have courses in high school to help girls, from the very start, know what to wear. What heartaches it would save them! And what money it would later save their husbands!

There are two things troubling the unsure woman. One is the problem of selecting the right costume for the right occasion; and the second is that she hasn't yet resolved in her own mind what her own special look should be. We will go into the "You Look" in a separate chapter because this is a subject which cannot be dismissed in a few words. It is too important. Women will spend hundreds of dollars to have someone tell them what is the right look for them. Many a woman spends that much for a single dress designed especially for her because a designer says, "This looks like you."

However, with a little training, any woman can decide exactly what is her own best look—just as Jacqueline Kennedy did. And if you will follow a few simple rules of appropriate dress, you can walk with confidence wherever you go.

For daytime, look chic and smart. Leave the elegant look for evening or for lounging in your home.

For the office wear suits and more suits, very simple dresses of casual, not glamor, weaves and appropriate materials—no silks or satins, but cottons, woolens, twills and tweeds, flat finished, dull surfaced materials. Don't even wear satin blouses for work. Knit garments, if not too figure-revealing, are all right in an office. Save the gleam and glitter for evenings, or at least for after five, the cocktail hour.

For work use necklines which reveal no cleavage. The arms should be covered, at least to the tip of the shoulder, even on hot days. This means that dresses with only straps over the shoulders are out. And sunback dresses have no place in an office, even in summer. Two-piece dresses are very good. Skirts may be slim, but never too nipped in. But if the skirts are loose, don't go to the other extreme and have them voluminous or bouffant. And, please, no multitude of petticoats. Dirndl effects are out of place in an office. And, of course, strapless tops are taboo—unless you're an attendant at a beach umbrella concession.

When Jackie went to work every day, she was ultra conservative. Her dresses in fall and winter had three-quarter length sleeves. She did not try to be a glamor girl— she avoided it. She wore casual dresses, shirtwaist dresses, coat dresses, skirts and sweaters and suits. She stayed away from dainty accessories for daytime. She carried a sizeable purse, wore comfortable looking medium-heeled pumps. No open-toed or fancy shoes for her. I never saw her wear a dangle earring for work. She wore small button earrings, if any. She wore single or double strand pearls, if any. She saved glitter and glamor for nighttime.

Only now and then did she wear a striking touch for daytime, as in the anecdote of the inscribed belt. That day she was going to a luncheon and, since it was summer, chose a Jackie-type, sleeveless, collarless, black daytime dress with the gold inscribed black belt.

This belt was a wonderful conversation piece, with its French inscription. But other than that, Jackie did not wear ornamentation such as bracelets and pins and lockets which served as "personal publicity." She did not wear heart-shaped jewelry in public. That would have stamped her with the label "little girl" or typed her as unsophisticated. For Jackie was sophisticated.

She never wore a slave bracelet on her ankle, nor a charm or dangling bracelet on her arm. She never wore anything like that for work, because objects which jangle can be distracting and draw attention to yourself—in a negative way. These may be worn for funtime, if you like, but not for work.

When you go to the office, don't look as though you're stopping in on your way to a party. One obstinate girl said to me, "I *want* to look that way; I want the other girls to envy me because they think I have a date right after work."

In my opinion, that girl is never going to have a date right after work with any nice fellow from her office because he won't want to support a girl who looks as though, for her, it's always party time.

Fortunately there are many ways you can cover a party dress. The best is to wear a two-piece outfit with a plain jacket in the office to cover bare shoulders or any glitter on the bodice.

The same rules apply for a woman going shopping in the city as apply to a girl going to work in an office. Simplicity and a business-like air should prevail. You should look efficient, as if you know what you want and how to get it. The salesgirls will respect you more for this. One woman told me that salesgirls always treated her in a slightly condescending way, made her feel they thought her scatter-brained. She wore party dresses for shopping, strapped evening sandals that revealed her stockings—or lack of them—a cocktail veil, spangles, many bracelets, not only choker beads, but choker beads that sparkled, matching drop earrings, and she jingle-jangled through her purchases. The salesgirls didn't look up to her. They probably felt they knew more about appropriate dressing than my customer did.

Office outfits can be made more colorful with a bright scarf which is casual, gay and feminine, but not distracting. You'd be surprised what effects you can achieve with a scarf. And have you ever worn a tiny fur or fur fabric scarf tucked into a plain wool dress? Very chic.

If you like a bit of sheen, it can be achieved with a patent leather belt and patent leather pumps. Jackie used this trick when she was an inquiring reporter. She would carry a black patent leather purse and wore black patent leather shoes with light-colored dresses in summer.

Gloves and purse should be unornamented and not too dainty, unless you are exceptionally small. Carry a purse large enough to hold all the things needed in a business day—a few small items bought while shopping, make-up and a pencil and notebook. This is not the time for the girl-of-leisure look.

You can get variation, too, in the patterns of the materials you wear. Jackie favored checks and gay plaids and interesting tweed textures. In summer she liked Indian madras and ginghams.

You can get away from monotony by wearing colored pumps and gloves with a neutral shade office dress or suit. A gray dress is a perfect foil for accessories with a touch of turquoise or shades of pink or red. Or try beige shoes and gloves with a plain, unadorned collarless black dress.

When Jackie was a career girl, she liked to match her purse and shoes. In summer she wore light browns and beiges, but she never wore white shoes. I agree that they are impractical for a career girl—hard to keep fresh and clean and, unless you have a size four foot, white shoes make your feet look big.

So now for daytime clothes, for shopping or the office, the rules are:

1. Simple suits and plain dresses in neutral solids, and not too bright plaids, checks, stripes and prints. Dull-textured materials only.

2. Non-shining jewelry. No dangling jewelry at ears, wrist or throat. Nothing that glitters in the office leads to gold—the simply dressed girl gets the raise.

3. Keep a simple, neat, uncluttered look. Keep accessories plain and neat.

4. Get color into your costume by bright accessories—scarf, gloves, purse or shoes. Don't get too many bright spots of color. One or two will do.

5. Beware! Do not show toes, even through stockings, or cleavage, even through peek-a-boo blouses.

6. If you wear a hat to the office or for shopping, it must be simple, not too large, fancy or decorated. And nothing sparkly, of course.

Going to a luncheon or tea?

The same rules apply at luncheon or tea time, in the White House or at a restaurant or the home of a friend.

The worst mistake is to wear a cocktail dress to lunch or brunch. Actually, a luncheon, even at the White House, requires a very simple daytime look, with only a hat to set it off.

A plain sheath dress with non-sparkling beads is fine. So is a simple suit which can be of silk, but not satin or brocade, nor any material shot with gold or silver threads.

In other words, if you are well-dressed for the office in a simple suit or solid-colored, plain black, conservative print or neutral colored dress, with neat pumps, a plain purse and clean white gloves, you are set for the White House. All you need add is a fine hat—the more colorful, the better. In spring, a White House luncheon looks like a garden of flowers, so lovely are the gay chapeaux the ladies wear. In winter, bright feathers are popular there, or hats made entirely of fur or feathers, or solid bright felts. Or the hat may be the color of the dress, but very dramatic and *distingué*.

So the rules for luncheon or tea time are much the same as the rules for office or shopping wear:

1. A simple suit or dress—not décolleté or full-skirted or bizarre in pattern.

2. No sparkle jewelry. Button earrings are best. One or two strands of beads, if any. Pearls are always right.

3. No fancy accessories. Plain pumps and purse and gloves. White gloves are best.

4. But you may wear the biggest, fanciest hat you want

to, to give color and dash to your costume. Or it may be not fancy at all, and still be very dramatic. Or it may be just a fragment of material matching your dress. But big or small, fancy, dramatic or plain, you *must* wear a hat. Even Jacqueline, who never cared for hats in the old days, bowed to custom and wore a hat to a White House luncheon when she was a Senator's wife. Now that she sets the pace as the First Lady, she always wears a hat for public appearances outside the White House.

At dusk, the cocktail hour:

Cocktail time is almost, but not quite, evening. As the custom has evolved in the United States, however, a woman may wear a cocktail gown for any evening party short of an Inaugural Ball or a formal affair where the men will wear white tie and tails and the women long dresses. There is no doubt about it, a long gown is the most elegant costume a woman can wear—and the most flattering and glamorous. It does the most for any woman.

In Paris and other European style centers, women jump straight from little daytime dresses into long elegant evening gowns. In America, women with leisure dress for cocktails and then change into a long gown for evenings. That is ideal, but not many can do it. In our democratic country, where few families now have servants, most women have to throw an apron around their cocktail dress and hurry to cook and serve their lord and master and the offspring, rather than change to a long evening gown. So the cocktail dress must do for the gala evening, too.

Cocktail time is the time of charm and now you may be completely feminine. Big, fluffy skirts are in. Or slinky sheaths. And décolleté. And cleavage. And laces. And little veils. And satins and brocades—the most elegant materials you can find. Go ahead and sparkle.

But before you sparkle in all directions, don't forget

the rules of elegance proclaim you must be discriminating. You can't be a hodgepodge and be elegant.

So you must decide just where you want to sparkle. If you are going to wear a terribly bright color, it will be more elegant to keep your dress unornamented and also not have too much sparkle in your accessories. Maybe just sparkling earrings. It is a wonderful trick of Jacqueline Kennedy's, when she wears an extravagantly styled gown, to wear only one splash of jewelry—chandelier earrings.

Or if you wear a sequin or lamé dress, it's better to wear no jewelry at all but, instead, to add a dash of the same color as your dress in a tiny veil on your head.

But remember the primary rule of elegance—restraint— still applies. Keep to a simple over-all design in your costume. If the dress material is very fancy, wear no jewelry at all—or simply little pearl earrings. Or sparkly earrings of the same color as your gown.

Here are my suggestions for cocktail dress:

1. You still need some kind of hat, or a little veil unless you are the hostess.

2. Wear a short, very dressy dress. But you must not have your shoulders completely bare. Your dress must have cap sleeves or wide shoulder bands. The scoop neckline, which Jackie likes, is very nice. The skirt may be slim or bouffant, as you like. Fluffy skirts of chiffon or other ethereal material, with heavier or shinier top of lamé or taffeta, are good. Or use the slim look of a Jackie-type sheath.

3. Cocktail suits are also excellent. Jacqueline likes these in brocade. The material keeps the suit from looking like a daytime outfit. The most lavish materials are tops.

4. Never wear long evening gloves for cocktails. Some lovely cocktail gloves are elegantly embroidered. But then soft pedal the rest of your costume.

5. Shoes may be as open as you please. If you like to count toes, now is the time for it. However, if you want to capture the elegance of Jacqueline Kennedy for yourself, notice that never does she turn toes up, even at cocktail time. She may wear satin slippers, but they are simple pumps with medium heels.

Your evening elegance:

Evening is any time after seven o'clock. This is the time for true elegance in the moonlight or under the soft glow of chandeliers, as only a long dress can make you elegant. With the long dress go long gloves—above the elbow.

As a general rule, an evening gown looks best when the front of the skirt is a trifle shorter than the back so that the toes of your shoes can peep out and you can trip the light fantastic with never a trip. The back of the skirt should be longer so the heels of your shoes don't show. However, sometimes a lovely effect is created by a gown that has an irregular hemline or one side sweeping up to show a shoe and ankle.

Of course, short evening gowns are also a part of the fashion picture today and some women find them less bothersome than long gowns, particularly in this age of the compact car. But they can never be quite as elegant. You can distinguish between a short evening gown and a cocktail dress by the shoulders and the accessories and, in some cases, by the materials. You might wear a dress of simple material for cocktails, but it would always be a fine, rich-looking material for an evening gown.

A cocktail gown always has some sort of shoulder covering or sleeves. An evening gown may be entirely strapless. But it doesn't have to be. Some of the most elegant gowns I have seen on Jacqueline have been bateau-necked, starkly simple, full-length sheaths, covered up and demure, actually, as a daytime dress. But always of elegant materials.

And with them she has worn fabulous, long earrings. Nothing more by way of jewelry or sparkle. Her shoes and purse are quite simple, plain and dainty.

So the rules for evening are:

1. The best, most elegant gowns are long and formed of the finest materials. But you may wear your dress long or short and sparkle if you choose.

2. Long gloves are obligatory and white ones are preferred.

3. Evening slippers are of brocade, satin, of gold, silver or embroidered leathers, or you may wear slippers custom-made of the material of your gown. Or you may wear evening sandals, especially with a gown designed on Grecian lines. Or peek-a-boo Cinderella slippers which have the transparency of glass and make you look as though you are dancing barefoot.

4. No hat, no veil. Only jewels in the hair or sparkling combs, ornamental hairpins or strings of beads woven through the coiffure.

5. An evening wrap or cape or furs should be worn or carried. An enormous wrap-around stole may be used.

6. Carry only a dainty evening bag of metallic material, fine leather or cloth, embroidered, jewelled or plain.

7. Wear evening stockings without reinforcement at toe or heel—called "barefoot" hose.

As I said, the rules are simple. If you stick to them and remember that, while gaiety and sparkle are right for certain times and places, even they must always be handled with restraint. Then you, too—whether your budget be low or high—can be as elegant as Jacqueline Kennedy. What more can anyone say?

CHAPTER 19

FROM FAULTS TO FAULTLESS

THE SECRET of Jacqueline's perfectly fitted clothes, before she was First Lady, was her use of a little dressmaker, not only to make dresses for her, but to improve those she bought in stores.

She even mentioned her little dressmaker during the Presidential campaign when people commented on how expensive her clothes looked. I am grateful that I was privileged to be that person in her life who altered "store bought" suits and dresses to fit as well as those I sewed for her.

Behind every lady of fashion, behind every social leader envied for her perfection of appearance, is a good "little dressmaker" who applies the finishing touches.

Even Marc Bohan, top designer of the House of Dior in Paris, admits that his wife still goes to her own little dressmaker. This doesn't mean she does not wear her husband's gorgeous creations. It only means that she is an individual with a few ideas of her own.

You would be amazed at what a little dressmaker can

do, if you are on a limited budget, to make your off-the-rack dresses look as though they were designed and made for you alone. Darts to take in fullness at the back of the neck if you are too rounded there. Elastics to keep a square neckline looking taut and perfect as in couturier gowns. Sleeves cut to exactly your most flattering arm length. Sleeves made more slender, or let out, to disguise underweight or overweight. And your dressmaker can make busts or hips look larger or smaller.

I'm sure you've seen women who go around with waistlines popping out above or below their belts. Some of them don't care and some don't realize that a little dressmaker could fix it. "If that's the way the dress was made, I guess that's the way it has to be," I've heard women say, with a fatalistic attitude. Such women are inclined to settle for second best all the way in life. Only if you demand perfection, do you get it.

Jacqueline often needed the waistlines of dresses lowered. If she hadn't had this done, the dresses wouldn't have looked nearly so well. She demanded perfection and never settled for second best.

And I'm sure you've heard women say, "Well, it's no use for me to try to look good. My neck's too short and *nothing* looks good on me." Or, "My legs are too thin. It's hopeless for me to try." Or, "My bust is too big" (or "too small"). Or, "I'm so short." Or, "I'm so tall I look like a walking bean pole."

There are many tricks of the trade—the dressmaking trade. There is even much that a dressmaker can pass along to you concerning your accessories. They can make or break your total look of elegance. Proportion is everything—well, almost everything. Color and whether to mix or match it is next. You can disguise your size with artful choice of purse and hat. The bigger the hat, the smaller you will look under it. Remember that. And the smaller the hat, the bigger you will look under it. The same goes for purses.

I remember a wonderful series the *Ladies' Home Journal* carried, which showed what happened when experts made over and modernized women through make-up and dress. The changes were fabulous, thrilling. So can yours be.

Facials give you a wonderful feeling and a relaxed expression, so why not use them? Fashionable young women do. One of Jackie's last appointments before the Inaugural Ceremony was for a facial. I used to go to the same beauty parlor in Georgetown which gave Jackie this news-making facial and I know how wonderfully relaxing their facials are.

All a designer can truthfully say is that, generally speaking, you should not repeat the shape of your face in your neckline or collar. If your face is too round, it can be made to appear less round by using straight lines and sharp angles in the neckline or collar. The sharp angle of a V or square neckline takes away the effect of the roundness—cuts the circle, so to speak.

And naturally the opposite is true. A long, sharply angular face gains an effect of softness by the placement of a softly curved neckline below it.

If you have a square face, you might do well to do as Jackie does—stay away from square necklines.

If you have an oval face, you can forget the shape of your face and wear any neckline you want *if* your neck is not too short and you don't have other figure problems.

Make your own experiments. Dare to let *yourself* give *you* the best advice. You *know* it is true and unvarnished and straight from the heart. It is not tinged with envy or malice or pity, or colored by what another woman would choose for herself.

A woman who is not trained in fashion is apt to think

that if a particular type of dress is right for her it must be right for every other woman and, in fact, she may think, subconsciously, there is something a little wrong with them if they don't wear what she wears.

Have you noticed how immature schoolgirls all tend to wear the same type of dress and look as though they were in uniform? Well, unfortunately, there are also schoolgirl-type women among your group of friends whom you can always spot because they look so *un*-individual, so afraid to really be themselves. Only the leader of this crew looks good in the "uniform." The others are just wearing it to feel safe and to gain approval.

Well, the truth of the matter is that it is no compliment to wear exactly the same dress someone else wears. More than once a First Lady has been caused great embarrassment when a guest arrived wearing a gown almost identical with that of hers. At one party Mrs. Eisenhower attended as First Lady she was faced with this situation. And in Paris Mrs. Kennedy had to switch dresses quickly when it became known that the one she had planned to wear was practically the same as the one another guest would be wearing.

First Ladies like to look *first*. Why don't you be a "First Lady" in your circle?

You can't be if you try to dress exactly like someone else. To begin with, you probably aren't the same height as she is. You may be taller, but there are certain advantages in every height.

If you are tall—as most models are today—you are probably the envy of all your friends. You are the one who can get away with bold prints, piles of chunky jewelry, huge hats, the new, wild, even clashing, colors—in other words, you can be the dramatic type. You are the one to introduce new ideas in clothes. Don't be ashamed of your height— carry yourself tall, *be bold,* carry the oversized handbag, wear large pieces of jewelry and lots of it, if you like, and convert YOUR LOOK into one of utter smartness.

If you are short, you have femininity on your side. Take the little things of fashion, the small bits of detail, and make them a part of YOUR LOOK. As for prints, the small, dainty ones are for you. A bit of color goes a long way. As to jewelry, use the dainty earrings and necklaces, not the overpowering ones. Small bracelets, or none at all. Or, in other words, scale all jewelry down to your proportions. Emphasize *you* rather than letting yourself be hidden behind large prints or too many clashing colors.

If you are average—or in-between—then you are the luckiest woman. With you, anything goes, depending on your mood. What may look overpowering on the little girl, or insignificant on the tall girl, may suddenly be just the right accent for you. Color, used with taste, can be the lift your clothes might need. Almost any print may be used and stripes are very interesting, horizontal or vertical. Jewelry is just a matter of your own taste, as long as it isn't too large or too small. In other words, fashion can be fun for you. Be imaginative and never let yourself get into a rut.

Now for your individual figure faults, make small adjustments to cover, to draw attention from, or to camouflage anything that doesn't look good to you, and you will go from fault to faultless.

If you are tall, but
have a good slim
figure —

You can wear extreme
and dramatic styles,
such as this kite
cape - coat with huge
buttons & pockets. You
can wear anything
big and bold and
high fashion.
Lucky you!

*If you are tall
but overweight —*

Wear loose flowing
garments till you take
off the excess weight.
Wear sharp-pointed
open collars and always
a line down the front,
with or without buttons.
Three-quarter length
sleeves are best. Avoid
round necklines and yokes

If you are tall,
but too thin —

Cover shoulder bones
and cut height with big
round collars. Ties add
bust fullness. If no collar,
wear lots of chunky
jewelry at neck. Wear
big skirts. Use big, wide
belts, if you like. Avoid
tight skirts and V necks

If you are too short, but have a good, slim figure

*Wear unbroken dress fronts to give height.
Do not wear too deep a neckline. Wear no
sleeves, or long slim sleeves. Wear no jewelry,
or small neat jewelry.*

If you are too
short and
overweight —

Wear vertical lines, such
as coat dresses. Wear open
collars of the same color.
No contrasting colors. Wear
hat of same color as dress
to add height, and shoes
to match, for same reason.
Little or no jewelry
at neck.

If you are too short and too thin ———

Wear full skirts and
softly rounded
necklines. Also softly
rounded shoulders,
covering shoulder
bone. Do not cut height
with wide contrasting
belts and avoid
V necklines

If you are medium
height, but slim —

You can wear dresses with special effects,
as long as they are scaled to your size.
Here is a dress designed to call attention
to lovely legs

If you are medium
height but overweight—

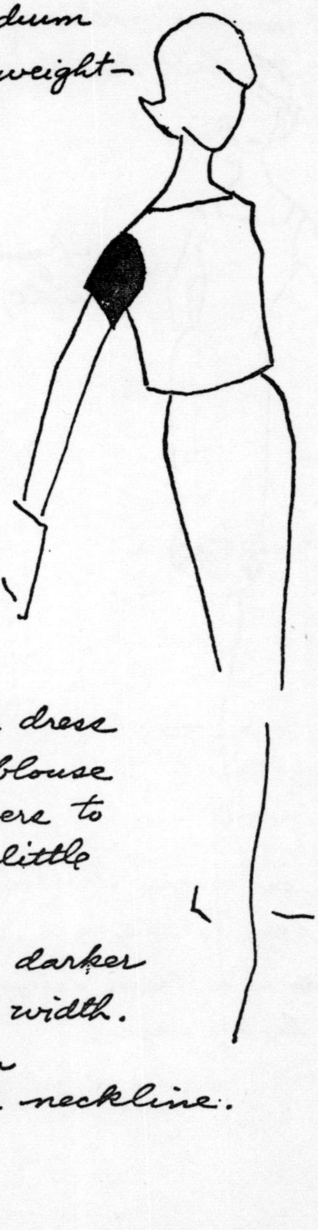

The two piece dress
and the overblouse
are life savers to
disguise a little
overweight.
Contrasting darker
sleeves cut width.
So does clean
uncluttered neckline.

If you are medium
height, but too
thin —

Wear rounded
high neck that
covers collarbone.
Wear interesting
full or pleated
skirts, like this
one in which there
are contrasting
printed inverted pleats

If you have a pointed chin ——

Wide square neckline

Soft patterns

round neckline

If you have a receding chin ——

low neckline

rolled collar

small prints

If you have a heavy chin ——

V neckline

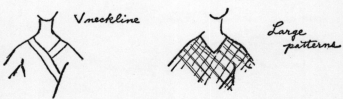

Large patterns

If you have a long neck

turtle-neck

choker on neck

standing collar

velvet ribbon

If you have a short neck

Open,
pointed-revere
collar

color contrast,
lighter at neck

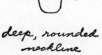

deep, rounded
neckline

scoop
neckline

If you have a double chin ⟶

Center attention
on hair & eyes

Plain neckline
Long beads

If you have lines in your neck ⟶

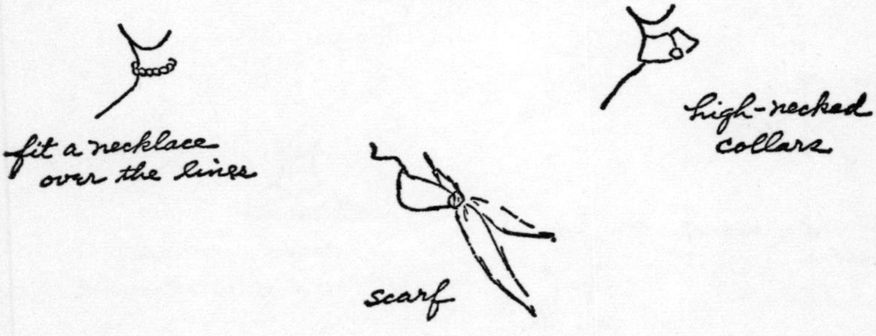

fit a necklace
over the lines

scarf

high-necked
collars

If you have square shoulders —

diagonal
shoulder
seams

dropped
shoulders

If you have sloping shoulders —

fichu

large collar

collar
standing
away from
neck

If you have thin arms —

always loose sleeves —

If you have long arms —

*3/4 length
sleeves
contrasting
glove*

*big
bracelets*

*puffed
sleeves*

If you have short arms

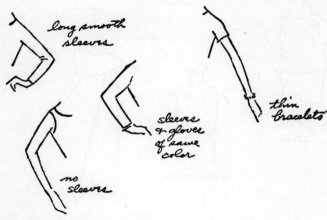

long smooth
sleeves

thin
bracelets

sleeves
+ gloves
of same
color

no
sleeves

If you have heavy arms
(always loose sleeves)

3/4 length
sleeves

short
flared
sleeves

dark
colors

If you have a sway back —

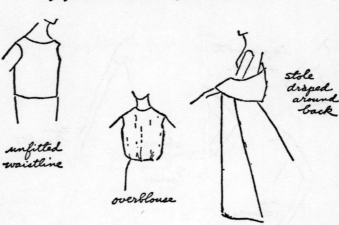

unfitted
waistline

overblouse

stole
draped
around
back

If you have a large rib cage —

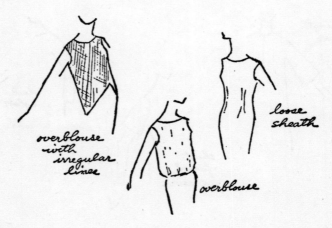

overblouse
with
irregular
lines

overblouse

loose
sheath

If you have a thick waist

overblouse

lines giving
illusion of slimness

loose,
lowered
waist

dropped waist

no belts
loose sheath

If you have a large abdomen —

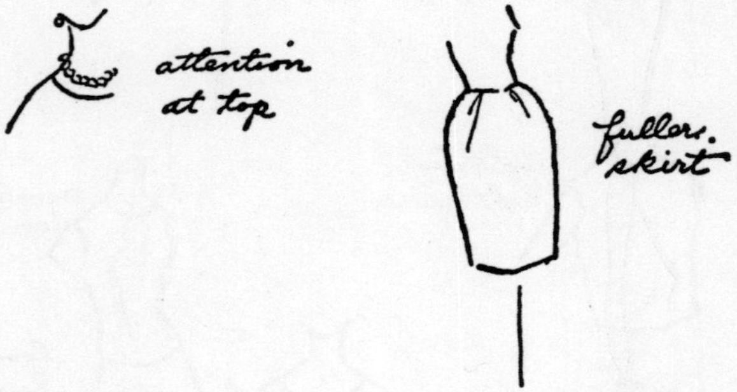

attention
at top

fuller.
skirt

If you have narrow shoulders —

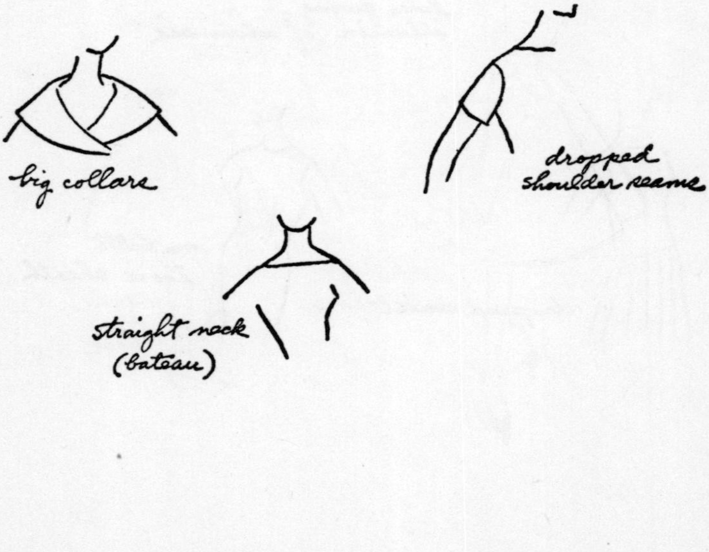

big collars

dropped
shoulder seams

straight neck
(bateau)

If you have thin legs

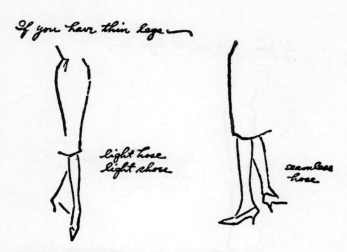

light hose
light shoes

seamless
hose

If you have heavy legs & ankles
(full, longer skirts)

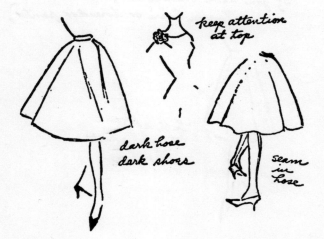

keep attention
at top

dark hose
dark shoes

seam
in
hose

If you have short legs

light hose & shoes
short skirts
high heels

If you have bowlegs
(never Capri or toreador pants)

full skirt
longer skirt
dark hose

If you have large hips

broaden shoulder line

keep attention at top

If you have thin hips

keep attention at top

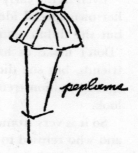

full skirts

peplums

CHAPTER 20

THE LESSON OF JACQUELINE

WHEN Jackie came to me to do her sewing, she was one of the few customers who didn't ask for a lot of advice. She accepted advice graciously—but usually ignored it. I was not insulted. I was happy about this because it meant that here was one woman who knew what she wanted—knew the look she was trying to achieve.

Even in the early Fifties, Jacqueline was working toward her own special identification. She was fond of her sister, but she didn't want to look or dress like Lee. She said, "Don't make us look alike." She had many fashionable friends, but she didn't try to copy them. She often went against fashion trends if they did not improve *her* special look.

So it is very ironic that now she, who was so independent and who refused to follow the crowd, is *being* followed by the crowd. Hosts of American women are ready to follow her fashion leads, whether her styles look good on them or not.

There is a big lesson to be learned here from Jacqueline. By every woman in America, actually—every housewife, every career girl, every young college student, and yes, even every high school girl.

And what worries me is that the lesson seems to be escaping a lot of women.

This lesson is a very personal one. It is for every woman to study herself and keep studying herself and then carefully work out every line and detail of a dress in order to make the most of her good features and express her personality. That's what Jackie did. It is to evolve her own look, a look which will not do for anyone else what it will do for her. She must find the one look—her own best look—that will make her stand out in a crowd.

If you are this woman, this alone will make you a leader. It is the quality of smartness and elegance which will make other, more timid women of your circle, follow your lead.

For the lesson of Jacqueline is: Find your own individuality—which is your own most important asset. Until you have found yourself, you can be blown about by conflicting advice from friends, relatives, and saleswomen, as unanchored as a leaf in the breeze. Only self-knowledge will give you roots to grow on and hold you firm in your convictions. Then you will be sure of yourself, and with self-knowledge comes serenity.

Jacqueline is so true to her own look and so true to herself that when she had a dress made by Givenchy in Paris—the dress that caused all the furor because she had broken her decision to wear only Cassini gowns—even the Givenchy dress had the Jackie stamp on it. It fitted right into her wardrobe. It was a slim, straight-lined, heavy white satin gown—slightly belled at the bottom. It had the uncluttered look which is her unique characteristic. As with some of her other gowns, the only ornamentation was some delicate embroidery on the bodice.

You may not be aware that you, too, have the potential for *your own* elegant look. You do. It may or may not resemble that of Jacqueline's. It all depends on how you look and how you *feel*. Because YOUR LOOK should be an outgrowth of your personality. It should express your viewpoint, your approach to life—yes, and even your dignity, your emotion or your sense of humor.

You may feel best in dresses that express great dignity. On the other hand, you may be at your best in bright-colored dresses which echo your sense of gaiety. There are even certain materials printed in humorous designs which make smart conversation pieces.

I think that Jackie's French-inscribed belt was an expression of her sense of humor, but her over-all look is of thoughtful dignity.

The actress who is most like Jacqueline Kennedy, even to the little sparkle of humor in her eyes, is Audrey Hepburn who, like the First Lady, presents a picture of thoughtful dignity in her mode of dress. Audrey Hepburn is, like Jacqueline, completely a lady, completely cultured, poised, self-possessed *and* completely an individual. She may vary her clothes a bit, and her hairdo, but, again like Jacqueline, she is always true in dress and hairdo to her own look. She is always Audrey, and for this audiences adore her and women study her clothes to learn her secret. I can tell them that her secret is knowing herself. That's why she always selects the right costumes for herself.

Blondes and brunettes can be equally elegant, but in a different way. There is the "Grace Kelly" look, which is a cool, blonde elegance, in contrast to the warm, dark Jacqueline Kennedy look.

It was a delight to see these two elegant beauties standing side by side at the White House to have their pictures taken with a Prince and a President. I thought to myself, who knows what great adventures lie ahead when you look different enough from the crowd to stand out?

You don't have to be a princess or a First Lady to be a

show stopper with your looks. But how, may I ask, can you stand out if you look like everyone else?

I'll never forget the evening I sat in a hotel dining room and saw a truly elegant woman make an entrance with her escort. She was all in ivory white—her gown and cloak in matching satin. There was a starkness and precision about her costume. Although the square neckline and wide straps over her shoulders were softened by a certain casual looseness of cut, a few soft folds over the bust had also been added by the designer for a relaxed line.

Her pale blonde hair was swept back and utterly simple, except for a bouffant effect on the top of her coiffure and a single strand of hair falling over her forehead, as if by accident. Her shoes and purse were of plain ivory satin.

The only exaggerated detail was a very wide necklace of about a dozen thin strands of cultured pearls, starting as a choker midway on her neck and descending gracefully in ever longer strands to halfway between her collarbone and her neckline. Other than that there was no ornamentation in the costume whatsoever. Even her earrings were merely small pearl buttons to match the pearls of her unusual collar necklace.

Everyone looked at her but her escort never noticed them. He was too enchanted.

As I studied her I thought, this picture in casual elegance could be painted in any century, at any time of history. Elegance, I reflected, is timeless.

And *you* will find, if you develop your own special look of elegance, that YOUR LOOK, too, will have a timeless quality. Photographs taken of you this year will be just as up to date ten years from now. For an elegant woman who has found herself, only the hemline changes.

In Washington, Mrs. Morris Cafritz is known not only as a top hostess but also for her elegance of appearance which has this timeless quality. Gwen Cafritz, who has been on the best-dressed list time and again, has her own look and is immediately recognized wherever she appears. Her trademark is her individual hair styling—long, black, luxurious hair, casually swept back into a bun. Very chic. Right for her and her dramatic clothes which reflect her dramatic hair style.

Also in Washington, Mrs. James L. Dixon is one of the most elegantly dressed women I have met, and the most simply dressed. No one has ever seen her in a bright color, yet there is a certain trimness which is arresting and reminiscent of the Duchess of Windsor—an underplaying of line and color. Yet those who know look at the deceptively plain clothes and know that simplicity is hard to achieve. Her trademark for evening is the evening muff, on which she pins her corsage—real flowers, of course.

A fashion supervisor, Lise Freeman, who is in charge of thirteen fashion departments at The Hecht Company in Washington, is known for her fantastic all-knit wardrobe. People stop her on the street to ask where she got her knitted dress and are amazed when she tells them it is four, or even ten, years old.

Recently she had some of her knits shortened, and, with the material cut off a turquoise one, had a new turquoise hat and bag made to match this dress and contrast with one of her black ones.

Lise, when she finds a knit style that is right for her, gets it with both long and short sleeves and in various colors. She has sleeveless knits, tailored knits, cocktail knits with deep cut fronts (one in black and white) and floor-length knit evening skirts, including a paisley print knit which she wears with a halter top. Some of the knits are Grecian in effect, some very sporty. Even her coats are knit and many match her dresses.

Now there's a girl who has used real originality to build a fabulous wardrobe and a fashion reputation while having fun. Collecting knitted dresses is her hobby. She collects them as others collect fine china. Friends join the treasure hunt.

Needless to say, the "knitted look" would come "undone" or "unravelled" on a heavy woman. Knits demand a slim, trim figure. So don't start knitting before you are sure you can wear your handiwork. There is also the question of how you feel in them. Although she works with all types of dresses every day, Lise feels happiest and most at home in knits. But would you?

Have you always worn a trim, uninspired, close-to-the-head hat because it's safe and inconspicuous? Well, it's time for a change. Go out and try on some hats that *are* hats. If you are large, or tall, try on some tremendous flower creations or a huge cartwheel or anything else sensational. Then wear it with an understated outfit, of course.

Fashion reputations have been built on hats. Hedda Hopper has become a living legend for her fabulous, extravagantly feminine hats. Others copy her—or try to.

In Washington, Alice Longworth, Teddy Roosevelt's daughter—who came once to my shop with a friend—has developed her look, the feature of which is her special type of broad, flat-brimmed hat. She is a picture of elegance—her own brand.

Eleni, the prize-winning fashion writer of *The Washington Evening Star,* has her own look, and little dark wings of hair at the cheeks set off by a special type of hat having a Mediterranean effect make her memorable. Unlike Hedda Hopper's, Eleni's hats are small, embroidered, uptilted beret types, many of them designed for her by Sally Victor.

Don Loper, the designer who dresses many Hollywood stars, endeared himself to me when he proclaimed that the most important thing a woman can learn about style is to say "No." In other words, she must pick her own look from a multitude of choices, and not be easily swayed.

Edith Head, another Hollywood designer and frequent

Oscar winner, has helped many a star discover "her look."
Starlets sent to her for the first time are atremble because
they know that what she can do for them may spell the
difference between a life as a bit player or stardom. Yet
what does Edith Head herself wear? She, who has every
trapping of glamor available to her?

I'll tell you. She puts on the simplest, most tailored
clothes you ever saw. *Her* look is the tailored look and,
with her trademark of straight-across black bangs, it's great.
You never have to think twice about which woman in the
room is Edith Head.

Mrs. Eisenhower had *her* look—appealing bangs and
mature, softly bouffant or flared skirts. I hold her in
greatest esteem for having saved American women from
the uniform harsh look of the bare foreheads of the
Forties. Most women, I find, look better with at least a
little twist or strand of hair over the forehead. But it took
Mamie Eisenhower, in the political campaign of 1952, to
give them, by example, the courage to wear bangs. And
believe me, it takes courage to be a front runner and take
the criticism that always follows in the wake of applause.

For that, the women of America owe her a great debt
of gratitude, just as they owe one to the new First Lady
for giving status to the released waist, the bare arm and
throat and the look of unbroken line.

I'm not asking you to change—to suddenly wear nothing
but knitted dresses, or nothing but black, or Mediterranean hats. I'm asking you to *find out who you are!* And
then you may want to change and you, yourself, may be
ready to change. Or you may not.

If your figure is truly curvaceous, you can't have the
Jackie look, but you can be another kind of show stopper.
As Zsa Zsa Gabor is. And blessings on her for her look of
enjoyment and pride at being a woman. Zsa Zsa Gabor

never looks like anyone else. She is a picture of utter femininity always.

You may find that you are happy with yourself as you are. That's great. It means you already know your best self. But isn't it time, if you haven't already done it, to find out *who* you truly are in spirit and whether you are expressing that self in your mode of dress?

American women have been accused of "buying a look" in the same way they buy a head of cabbage or a grapefruit at the supermarket. But YOUR LOOK is not an ordinary commodity that anyone can buy at "three for a quarter."

You can develop a fashion personality and be known for some special touch in your costume—sheer black stockings with a black dress. Or witches' hats. Or flowered gloves. Or coats belted in back and voluminous in front. Free your mind. Have fun with clothes.

Get the Parisian slant on fashions. In America clothes are a chore. In France they are a hobby.

What would you like to be known for? What makes you feel good all over?

That is the YOU LOOK.

One of the best investments you can make is to subscribe to several women's magazines—those devoted to fashion exclusively and the general feature ones such as *Good Housekeeping*, the *Ladies' Home Journal* and *McCall's* which give you a balanced fare. Reading them can help you greatly in developing a knowledgeable and fashionable you.

Read *Vogue, Glamor, Mademoiselle, Harper's Bazaar*—and even one of the exciting French fashion magazines. You need these magazines to expand your horizon and help you see the big fashion picture. Not as a copycat, mind you, but for adaptation or variety, for fun, for self-expression, for confidence and for helping you understand the *better* you.

CHAPTER 21

HOW TO DEVELOP THE *YOU* LOOK

Now LET's talk about YOU.

You've read the rules of proper dress—what to wear when and where—they were simply to give you ease of mind and a feeling of confidence in knowing you are properly dressed.

You have read the rules of design and proportion—what general rules to follow to look well integrated. And you've seen sketches which suggest what you can do to look free of figure faults. These, too, are simply your guides.

But now there is one final step in developing your clothes sense, and that concerns the art of self-expression. First, let's find out what the mirror says when you stand before it. What is the general impression? What does the picture in the mirror seem to say?

Write down just how you impress yourself. What is the message that girl in the mirror seems to convey? WRITE IT DOWN. This is no time for modesty or conceit or embarrassment. If you face yourself *now*, you may change your whole future.

Now, when that is done, ask yourself one question: "What do I *wish* my double were saying to me?"

WRITE THAT DOWN. Put it down in one paragraph. This is your moment of truth. No pretense is necessary because only *you* will read it. You may find that, without any smugness, you are satisfied; you like being the type you are. Or you may find you like being a little pixie and you want to emphasize that look. Or you may want to emphasize a young-clubwoman-with-children-at-home look.

You may want to look like a temptress and, if you do, then you will feel right to go out and buy a tiger skin printed blouse or scarf. And you will feel good now to dare wear slinky clothes and lots of black—maybe even for evening a black sequin sheath from chin to floor.

Ah, but the trouble comes in when you, the pixie type, want to look like the temptress. Or the outdoorsy girl wants to become the pixie. Now we have a problem to resolve. Can you switch from one personality to another? Usually YES!

Of course you can. It's done every day. My favorite illustration for how someone showed this complete change in self-expression and fashion personality is Doris Day. Remember the Doris Day of old, with the cleanly scrubbed girl-next-door look—hair tousled over forehead, clothes casual, and the roles in her movies were of this type? Then, suddenly, in a movie called "Midnight Lace," remember the new Doris Day who emerged—sultry and desirable, with long high fashion gowns to match and a longer glamorous hairdo, a little bouffant but straight back from the forehead and coming to little upside-down question marks out from the sides?

She had made a complete transition and it was sensational.

My conviction, from years of working with women in the intimacy of the fitting room, is that it is more important for a woman to become the woman she feels she really is and yearns to express than to try to live up to or down to some external feature that can be toned down or changed.

Most women dress the way they do not to express their own personalities but to please some relative—mother, husband or even child. I see red when I hear a grown woman say she would love to have a certain dress but she is afraid her *daughter* would *disapprove.*

One woman I knew dressed all in fluffy ruffles and hated it. But she was afraid to change because that was the *girl* her husband had fallen in love with! She was still striving, thirty years later, to be the girl her husband had first met and, in doing so, she had stifled her adult personality.

You will gain such new enjoyment of life as you've never dreamed if you will let your own personality shine through to other people, and not let your clothes bespeak an alien personality.

Let me tell you of two women I know who were quite unhappy with their lot in life until they changed their form of self-expression in their clothes.

One of them was lighthearted and gay, but dressed very somberly because her husband was very dignified and conservative. Her muddy colors made her look dismal and she was always complaining, "I never have any fun. I love bright prints but I'm afraid my husband wouldn't approve of them."

The other woman yearned for people to treat her with greater respect. But naturally they took their cue from her clothes and treated her like a child because her clothes were childish—almost ridiculously so—little girl collars and tiny bridesmaid hats and lots of color and prints, and big belts and fluffy skirts. They looked anything but dignified. Had she been going to high school she would have been chosen as the "most darling" in the year book. Her husband was very wealthy, incidentally, but I noticed he didn't take his "child wife" to official dinners if he could help it.

Both of these stories have happy endings. Slowly I felt my way about explaining to each—privately, of course—how I saw their clothes problem and eventually both did a complete turn about face—one overnight, one over a year's time. These women never even met, but I like to reflect on how, to a degree, they exchanged clothes personalities.

Each, when she was dressed in the clothes that gave her self-assurance, became the person she really felt she was and thus a truer personality—a person to whom others responded more readily.

The first woman started wearing her "bright prints" and gay patterns. She became more vivacious and animated with the encouragement her clothes now gave her. People responded to her new show of warmth—which they expected because of her new colorful look—and she told me countless times how people were singling her out to tell her the latest joke or anecdote and how happy she was. She reveled in exploring her true personality. Her husband, too, responded by listening eagerly to the new stories she was bringing home to relate to him.

The second woman became dignity personified in her dress—neat, slim skirts, sophisticated, collarless necklines or fold-back collars, sober colors. Sophisticated jewelry. Goodbye "little girl." This change in dress had a wonderful effect on her and the people around her. They saw her innate dignity for the first time and they responded by treating her with a certain deference. Her posture became better as her confidence grew and it came to pass that her husband proudly introduced her to his business associates. I know because I made her a most glamorous banquet gown and a chic outfit for travel.

So we must face the fact that in order to make people

treat us the way we want to be treated we must express
our inner self in our outward appearance.

The more dignified our dress, the more will we be
treated with dignity.

The more happy-go-lucky our clothes, the more casual
will be their approach to us.

If we want to have a come-hither look, our clothes must
say, "Come hither."

If we want to make men feel protective toward us, our
clothes must have a delicate, fragile and feminine air that
says, "Come take care of me."

It fascinated me to see the evolution of my two daughters—Sylvia into a look of serene dignity, and Jimi into a
siren look. The man who responded to the Siren Look was
a conservative engineer who enjoyed seeing the attention
Jimi got. The man who responded to the Quiet Look was
a noted sports car racer who is not afraid of the lime-
light and likes Sylvia's dignified reticence. Sylvia, in her
quiet colors, is the one who enjoys his limelight.

So the needs of both girls have been fulfilled because
they dressed to show their true selves. I have noticed that
couples who are competitive, fashionwise or any other way,
are not the most happy. So dress to your true self and help
the right man recognize *you* when he finds you.

My own look expresses, I hope, a certain gaiety. I like
black dress suits with gay flowered linings, and blouses of
material matching the lining. The black suit suggests a
certain dignity but the colorful print says, "Come, let's
talk a while. Let's enjoy a lively, lighthearted conversation."

I like hats that stand tall and perky and are made of
material matching that of my outfit, in order to give me
height and draw attention away from my weak chin.

I hope my look is the "I'm-interested-in-you" look.

Your look is the look which best reflects your most

prevailing mood—the expression of your basic personality as modified by God-given features, such as size, coloring and figure. It is the look which captures the flavor of your interests and way of life. It tells whether you are gay and fun loving. Or serious. Or active. Or stay-at-home. Or dramatic. Or serene. Or modest. Or extravagant. Or clinging. Or restful. Or tempestuous. Or thoughtful. Or what have you?

In order to help you develop the style which you have chosen to suit your personality, I am going to give you a suggestion as to how you can achieve this. You will need to see your proportions as though you were looking at a statue.

For this you will need to drape your unclothed body in muslin so you will get the total effect of your proportions and body outline without the distraction of underwear or clothing. Also without the distraction of color, because unbleached muslin is neutral.

And, finally, because it is inexpensive, you can buy enough extra muslin to pin additional pieces on, using the form-fitting base to pin to—in order to see yourself with every possible type of variation of line and design.

Take a piece of muslin twice the length of the distance from your shoulders to the floor. Fold it in half and make a small opening for the head. Put it on. Pin the shoulder seams to conform to the slope of your shoulders. Let the muslin fall naturally over your body. Before starting any darts, the two sides should be pinned together down each side just enough to hold them in place somewhat near the body.

Now pin the bust darts on each side, starting from under the arm and pointing to the fullest part of your bust. Make the waist darts, starting just below the two breasts and going to the waist. Just under the bust darts, at the waist, taper them downward to make darts over the curve of your stomach.

In back make small darts on each side, up from the waistline and longer ones below the waist. Sometimes you may need more darts to adjust to your figure. If your figure is an hourglass, make two darts on each side.

If you are round-shouldered, pin a small dart on each side in back of the bodice, in the center of each shoulder.

If you are full-busted, put darts in front on each side of the bodice at the center of the shoulders, just opposite the back darts, if you have darts. A person who needs a back dart generally needs a front shoulder dart, also.

The muslin should fit like your second skin. This is, incidentally, also the way you can check your dimensions against the standard patterns you buy, in order to make your clothes fit better. It is hard to fit the muslin on yourself and it is much easier if you get a friend to help.

Take a pencil and draw a line at the natural waistline all around your body. Re-check your pinning on each side of the body, so the muslin fits snugly.

For the armholes, cut around the arm from the rounded part of your shoulder and under the armpits. Be sure to cut them large enough so you are comfortable.

Pin the side seams snugly from under the arms to the floor, leaving just room enough to walk.

Before you forget, right now, wherever the pins are, draw lines on the cloth with a soft pencil, on both sides of the pins.

Finally, pin all the loose edges back close to the skin so that you now stand in a muslin second skin which gives you a chance to really see and study the outline of your figure and also gives you a base on which to start pinning material to see for yourself what various effects do *to you* and *for you.*

Now you must experiment like a scientist. Yes, like a

truth-seeking scientist. Experiment with what various shapes and colors do for you. Cut a peplum and see what it does for your hips. Cut various necklines and hold them against you to see what happens to your face. Fold the hem at various lengths and see what hemline is ideal for you. Cut various shoulder effects and see what they do for you.

To make lines stand out, use an artist's grease pencil. Get the effect of a line down the middle. Do you look better with an unbroken front as Jacqueline does? How about her necklines? Are you better off with a deep-cut neck? A sweetheart neck? Scallops? Square? Scoop? Bateau? Try a loose-fitting released waist. Are straight lines for you? Pin on a skirt with a flare. How is that?

The mirror is the witness and you are the judge. So rely on *yourself* first and foremost.

Now do the same for colors. Get out scarves and dresses of every color in the rainbow and a few that aren't—like black and navy—and drape them around your neck and shoulders. Study yourself. Which look good on you, which don't? Be brutal. If red makes your complexion look like raw liver, cast it from you and remember that picture of yourself in red when next some salesgirl is telling you, "This red would look lovely on you, Dear."

I remember a young friend of Jacqueline's who said, "This color looks like an illness." I studied the color and it was a sickening hodgepodge of all colors and looked like no color under heaven. It was a neutral green-gray—if that is possible. And on her, it did look like an illnes. She didn't have the dress made after all. She just took the material back to the store and paid the penalty of not getting full money back. Because why throw good money after bad?

I've known a lot of women who tried to justify keeping a dress and spent more money than it was worth trying to make it wearable, using new accessories, for example, and it still didn't look good on them. One woman said, "If it kills me, I'm going to prove to my husband that I look good in pink." And it almost did kill her looks.

She had thought that because Jacqueline Kennedy, who has dark chestnut hair, looks good in hot pink, so should she. Well, she was wrong. This customer, who was a decided blonde, looked like a double-dip ice cream cone— two flavors, lemon and strawberry. And who wants to eat ice cream all day? Especially that combination. That's about what her husband had said, but she wouldn't believe him.

When I put her in front of the mirror and showed her how "gooey" she looked with her particular shade of hair against bright pink, and then held cooler colors, which did look good, up around her neck for her inspection, she thanked me for showing her, and decided she'd just let Jacqueline be Jacqueline and she would be she.

"I got carried away," she said. "I was not really seeing *me* in the store." Not all blondes look good in pink. And there are pinks and pinks. Jacqueline knows which are good on her.

Actually, this woman looks best in black which permits her lovely hair to be the major attraction of her lovely self. She looks elegant when playing down all other colors. Her own coloring is good. Hot pinks make her look florid. So for a change from black, she uses grays, the cooler blues and pale green.

On the other hand, one redheaded customer had the courage to buy a Jacqueline pink dress and on *her* it looked ravishing. She is including a lot of hot pink in her wardrobe.

Color is a psychological factor and even if some colors look good on you and everyone tells you to wear them, don't pay any attention to them, if wearing them is a torture to you.

One of my customers, another redhead, had been dressed in Kelly green as a child. Head to hem, she wore green—coats, hats, the works. All green. And for shoes, brown had been decreed by her mother. The green had achieved the mother's purpose of making her daughter's hair look redder, but the poor girl had grown to hate the bright color and has never worn it since she has been coming to me. "I got so I wondered if I was fading into the shrubbery," she said. "And I even wished leaves of trees would turn blue, I was so sick of seeing green."

I feel little girls, from early childhood, should be permitted to pick their own colors, within reason. I once talked to a psychologist about this and he agreed. It is part of letting a girl develop her own personality.

I give Mrs. Auchincloss a lot of credit for the fact that both Bouvier sisters, Jacqueline and Caroline Lee, are among the best-dressed women. She was the best mother they could have—teaching them the things they needed to know for confidence, such as when to wear gloves, and what type to wear, but then letting them have a free hand in deciding on their own styles and encouraging them to grow "fashion wise."

Jacqueline did not become a fashion leader or pace setter overnight. She evolved slowly, just as I am sure she will continue to do. Those who follow her slavishly will learn that the "Jackie look" they started out with has altered and is not the "Jackie look" of the moment.

The only way to follow her leadership is to perfect your own look and develop from year to year—not over a weekend.

And when you find your look, or some of the features which you realize your look should contain, hold on to those features, repeat them over and over in dresses with slight variations. I have seen dozens of necklines on the First Lady which are all "Jackie" types, but each was slightly different, coming a little closer or farther away from the shoulder blade, being a little straighter or bateau, or a little more scooped, or now and then coming down just a trifle from the shoulder and then making a straight line across the front. And the skirts varied too, sometimes tighter, sometimes cut by a few box pleats, sometimes higher or lower waisted, sometimes without waist indicated at all. But they always still had the "Jackie look."

At this stage in her development, Jacqueline feels best in a dress with a flat, unbroken front panel. True, there may be some embroidery or slight ornamentation, but the effect is almost that of a whole piece of cloth held up on her, sometimes shoulder to floor, sometimes shoulder to knee and sometimes, for a two-piece effect, shoulder to hip. On her it is stunning, fantastically chic. But if you are full-busted, this may make you look larger and even somewhat like a farmer's bag of meal, stuffed but unshapen.

Only wear what looks good on *you*.

You can call it a return to the Grecian, or Egyptian, or the Roman, or the cave girl. Whatever you do, don't be afraid. Some other designer has already thought of it. Some other fashionable woman has already worn it. Wide, wide suit jacket—slim skirt? Chanel developed it. The straight, unwaisted dress is in the tradition of Givenchy who gave us the sack look for a "new dimension." The look of extreme length or shortness? Dior.

But here is a word of caution. My rule is to be brave and individual in every dress detail but the length. Vary your length only an inch or two from prevailing fashion. Nothing dates a woman more than to wear very long dresses when everyone else has them very short. Skirt lengths seem to make drastic changes about every seven years. From very short to very long, or from very long to very short. So every few years you'll have your own best length style.

Now, of course, you must be reasonable. You must be influenced by your size in developing your look. Dainty, tiny hats or purses on a large woman are ridiculous, just as huge hats or purses or patterns that dwarf a tiny woman are ridiculous.

Keep to scale. Never, never buy the wrong size accessory just because you *like* it. You have to keep looking until you find one you like in your size. Or, in the case of hat and purse, have them made or make them. But you can still express your true disposition and personality, no matter what your size.

You can be tall and still develop a gentle look. You don't automatically have to develop a bold look. But you *do* have to be bold in selecting larger objects as accessories to go with your larger than average frame.

Career and college girls are forever asking me what clothes to wear to "catch a man."

If you wear the clothes which express the things you are, you will attract the man who will respond to your special personality like a magnet. A man who wants to take care of a woman responds to the fragile feminine look. A man who admires the outdoor woman responds to the casual look. A man who enjoys basking in reflected lime-light likes to make an entrance with a woman who looks like an actress. A very distinguished man looking for his equal will gravitate to the woman who displays her dignity in her clothes and he will thank his lucky stars he found her.

And yes, some brave, strong man will surely step forward to tame the tiger!

There is actually something a little "phony" looking about a woman who is one type and is trying to look another. It just doesn't ring true and men are wary of pretense.

But while you are developing *your* look, never lose sight

328 / I Was Jacqueline Kennedy's Dressmaker

of the basic rules of elegance because you are, after all, searching for the *most elegant "you look."*

Remember the real *you look* has a timeless quality because it is so right. So basic. So true. It presents a perfect picture.

It is the picture of *you.*

EPILOGUE

JACKIE IS IN the White House now—gone from Merrywood and Georgetown—and I am gone from Washington. And yet, I return again and again to the old haunts. In fact, it is amusing to me that now I am doing something she once did—making squiggle drawings of dress ideas and taking them to Washington every few weeks for daughter Sylvia to help me put them into finished fashion designs.

I am grateful to be still a part of Washington. Not only do I have the pleasure of working as a team with my daughter—see the sketches in this book—but I have a chance to feel a part of the Washington scene and to keep track of White House news.

Some people are bird watchers. I am a White House watcher and I savor every experience of driving past the Executive Mansion. Then I feel happy for Jacqueline that, to quote Letitia Baldrige, her social secretary, she is "the girl who has everything, including the President of the United States."

Now and then I run into people who knew Jackie *then* and I am transported back in time through a chain of memories to those earlier years.

And always the news has a reminiscent ring—the President having more back trouble, for example. I remember when Jackie was worried about his back even before they were married.

And I hear that the First Lady deplores the emphasis on her clothes just as I recall her doing when she refused to put clothes first in her life by deciding not to work for *Vogue*. But what can she do when all of France is still talking about her visit and adapting a bit of the "Jackie look" themselves? Also the Japanese have paid tribute to her good taste by presenting her with a bolt of golden cloth on the occasion of the visit of Prime Minister and Mrs. Hayato Ikeda to Washington, so that she may design and have made either an evening gown or a cloth-of-gold evening wrap.

Do what she will, she is now an international fashion figure. Nothing she can do can change that.

I hear that Jackie hasn't forgotten her old crowd at the *Times-Herald*. One of the photographers, Joe Heilberger, was covering the Kennedy family at Hyannis Port and Jacqueline said to her daughter, "Go smile for Joe. He used to work with Mummy."

I think Caroline is starting to understand about "Mummy's" career. I think her life is perhaps a little enriched when Jackie tells her of those interviews—what the dogs at the veterinarian's told Mummy and how dogs live on shipboard when they go abroad, and what the little children, the many little children, told her about life and school and Santa Claus and who is "badder"—girls or boys.

Caroline, like her mother, has become a great animal lover, with a menagerie of ducks and fish and a pony named Macaroni and a canary named Robin and a hamster named Debbie and a kitten named Mitten and a dog named Charlie and another pup with a strange Russian name Pushinka, because it came from Russia—and an occasional imaginary animal thrown in for good measure.

Yes, I hear Caroline is absolutely a chip off the old block. Just like her mother, even to being absolutely frank and honest and open with everybody. For example, she asked the ultra-dignified House Speaker Sam Rayburn point-blank why he didn't have hair on his head.

And talk about aplomb! Caroline certainly has her mother's poise. The first thing she said when she almost drowned in her step-aunt Nina's swimming pool, and a woman jumped in fully dressed and saved her, was, "Why do you have all your clothes on in the water?"

I hear that Jacqueline is saving the little stories she makes up for Caroline and illustrates with her own squiggle drawings. I hope that some day she will let them be published and share them with all the children of America.

It was a happy time for me when the Women's National Press Club, of which my co-author is a member, produced a skit in which members played the rolls of the "New Frontiersmen" and the White House family. The main character on stage was "Caroline," played by Bonnie Angelo of *Newsday,* who sat on a tricycle all through the acts, making typical Caroline comments.

Those who sat close to the First Lady at this affair, which took place at the Statler Hilton Hotel in Washington, said that some of the punch lines delivered by "Caroline" in baby treble hit home so well that Jacqueline hid her face in her program:

"Sometimes my Daddy sits around with his shoes off doing absolutely nothing . . .

"My Mommie's 31 and wears an 8½ shoe."

Jacqueline found herself being depicted by dark-haired, glamorous, pressgirl Deena Clark of *Diplomat Magazine.* She recited the words of a poem written by a committee headed by Christine Sadler of *McCall's:*

JACQUELINE'S LAMENT

> I first met Jack at a small soirée
> With Georgetown friends while out to play
> He talked politics night and day! . . .

For two whole years before we wed
The life of a working girl I led
Just to prove that I could get ahead! . . .

If I had known then what I know now,
About that Boston heir
I'd have studied Walter Lippmann
And forsaken Molière . . .

Oleg Cassini designs clothes for me.
I've even had Balanchine for tea,
DeGaulle called out the fleet for me . . .

Paris says my hat is in!
They're even naming roses Jacqueline.
The world takes to my every whim . . .

We went one day—my co-author and I—to all the places where Jackie walked the town with her camera.

The house where Jackie came with imported material for a new dress is still there, but oh, the changes that have been wrought! Now 1820–35 Street, N.W., has been painted a fashionable beige and now the vacant lot next door is gone, and with it the big tree. And in its place is another fashionable and quaint flat-front Georgetown house. The dogwood was in bloom. But it was still not quite the tree I had envisioned. And the shrubbery has now taken over the yard, as if to make up for the dogwood's laziness.

Gordon Junior High was letting out and a bunch of boys ran by in school sweaters. I thought how sad it was that they didn't know how Jackie's car used to stand there in earlier years and how the boys used to swarm over it, waiting for Jackie to come out. How they adored her and wouldn't let her go on her way! And where is the boy who came with an idea for her column—too late? Grown up by now—but what is he doing? And does he realize his camera girl became the First Lady?

We looked conspicuous standing there like insurance adjusters. So we walked away, past the corner grocery store. No limousines standing there now. We walked around the corner and another and another until we were in the many-fenced alley where we could peep through and see the back of the house.

Ah, what a wonderful atmosphere pervades a Georgetown alley—all patios and climbing ivy and splashes of flowers and old Greek statuary and quaint bird baths. The alleys of Georgetown are like none other. We saw the patio outside my old sewing room French doors. Through those wide-flung doors I had sniffed the spring. Through those doors had come the little boys who had tried to design a dress on my model, using Jackie's material. I shuddered as I thought of it. Where were the flowers I had smelled? Where was the happy time?

We hurried away and downtown to 13th and H Streets, N.W. The old *Times-Herald* Building looked sad now— all boarded up and closed and no amount of knocking would bring anyone to open the heavy door. I remember when the door was always open and the windows brightly lighted, and Jackie hurried in and out. And the little restaurant, where she went for coffee for the city room, is closed. No business there. I could almost hear voices ring out, calling to Jacqueline, "How was the shooting today? Anyone get away?"

Gone. Gone. All gone.

And the very name of the newspaper is gone. The Washington *Times-Herald* was bought by *The Washington Post,* and at first the name "Times-Herald" was big and bold on the *Post's* masthead and then it shrank and shrank and now it is very tiny as it sits sedately under the name of *The Washington Post.* A shadow of its former flamboyance remains to remind me of things past.

But those two words, "Times-Herald," are all I need for

remembrance. And I am sad when I think that only the older Washingtonians can remember and appreciate what colorful events those words summon up.

I want to capture forever a picture of the earlier Jacqueline. I don't think we should lose sight of the tall slim girl with the heavy camera and the big shoulder purse and the French fashion magazines and the shirtwaist dresses and the merry laugh and the twinkling light brown eyes, who pounded the sidewalks and stopped people and asked the questions and made the notes and wrote the column and waited for her by-line—because now this picture of her belongs to history.